MILITARY HISTORY FROM PRIMARY SOURCES

LESSONS FROM VIETNAM
Ia Drang And Other Battles
THE ILLUSTRATED EDITION

BY JOHN A. CASH, JOHN ALBRIGHT
AND ALLAN W. SANDSTRUM

EDITED BY
BOB CARRUTHERS

CODA
BOOKS LTD

This book is published in Great Britain in 2013 by
Coda Books Ltd, Office Suite 2, Shrieves Walk, Sheep Street, Stratford upon Avon,
Warwickshire CV37 6GJ.
www.codabooks.com
Copyright © 2013 Coda Books Ltd

ISBN 978-1-78158-362-3

A CIP catalogue record for this book is available from the British Library.
All rights reserved. No part of this publication may be reproduced or transmitted in any form or by any means electronic or mechanical, including photocopy, recording, or any information storage and retrieval system, without the prior permission in writing from the publisher.

This book was first published by the Department of the Army, Washington D.C in 1970 as 'Seven Firefights in Vietnam', and was written by
John A. Cash, John Albright and Allan W. Sandstrum.

CONTENTS

Foreword 5

The Authors 6

Preface 7

1. Fight At Ia Drang 9

2. Convoy Ambush On Highway 1 49

3. Ambush At Phuoc An 66

4. Fight Along The Rach Ba Rai 74

5. Three Companies At Dak To 92

6. Battle Of Lang Vei 117

7. Gunship Mission 148

Glossary 163

Foreword

The Center of Military History is again pleased to reprint Seven Firefights in Vietnam, the first of any kind of publication under the Center's imprint to appear on this conflict.

The events described in this small book are illustrative of much that took place in Vietnam after American troops were first committed in force in 1965: of heroic achievement and sacrifice, of human error, of experimentation and innovation, of a wily and elusive enemy, and of a new dimension in warfare afforded by the helicopter.

These accounts serve as a preliminary record of the achievements of men who served their nation well, a preface to a full military history of the war that is in preparation. The narratives also serve as valuable lessons to soldiers pursuing lessons of small unit actions.

Washington, D.C., 11 October 1984
DOUGLAS KINNARD
Brigadier General, USA (Ret.)
Chief of Military History

The Authors

John Albright served in Vietnam as a captain in the 11th Armoured Cavalry Regiment and participated in the action, "Convoy Ambush on Highway 1." He received the B.A. degree from Oklahoma State University and is engaged in graduate study at The American University. He has served two short terms in Vietnam as a civilian historian while employed in the Office of the Chief of Military History.

John A. Cash, Major, Infantry, an experienced officer, served in Vietnam as a company commander and as a member of a brigade operations staff in the 1st Cavalry Division (Airmobile), in the latter capacity participating in the action, "Fight at Ia Drang." He also served two short tours in Vietnam as a historian on special missions for the Office of the Chief of Military History, to which he was assigned from 1966 through 1968. On the second short tour he was involved in the action, "Gunship Mission." Major Cash holds the B.A. and M.A. degrees in history from Rutgers University and the M.A. from the University of Wisconsin.

Allan W. Sandstrum, Lieutenant Colonel, Field Artillery, served on the G-3 staff of I Field Force, Vietnam. He received the B.A. degree from the University of California at Los Angeles and the M.A. degree in history from the University of Texas at El Paso. Colonel Sandstrum is currently assigned to the Office of the Chief of Military History.

Preface

These accounts of fighting in Vietnam are based upon official U.S. Army records—daily journals, journal files, and after action reports; upon interviews conducted soon after the events by historical officers in Vietnam; and upon interviews and correspondence conducted later by the authors themselves. Although no documentation is included in the published work, a fully annotated copy of the manuscript is on file in the Office of the Chief of Military History.

The editor for the volume was Loretto C. Stevens; the copy editor, Barbara J. Harris. Photographs were selected, with the assistance of the authors, by Ruth A. Phillips. Maps were prepared in the office of The Adjutant General. The undersigned exercised general supervision over the preparation of the studies.

Washington, D.C., 25 March 1970
CHARLES B. MacDONALD
Deputy Chief Historian for Southeast Asia

Map 1. South Vietnam, locations of the seven firefights.

1. Fight at Ia Drang
14-16 November 1965

BY JOHN A. CASH

Up to the fall of 1965 the fighting by U.S. troops in Vietnam had been characterized, for the most part, by hit-and-run counterinsurgency operations against Viet Cong irregulars. It was during the week before Thanksgiving, amidst the scrub brush and stunted trees of the Ia Drang River valley in the western sector of Pleiku Province along the Cambodian border that the war changed drastically. For the first time regular North Vietnamese regiments, controlled by a division-size headquarters, engaged in a conventional contest with U.S. forces. The 1st Battalion, 7th Cavalry, 1st Cavalry Division (Airmobile), took the lead in this battle.

North Vietnamese General Chu Huy Man's Western Highlands Field Front headquarters had conceived a bold plan for operations in the Central Highlands of the Republic of Vietnam. To be carried out in the fall of 1965 and designated the Tay Nguyen Campaign, the enemy plan called for an offensive against the western plateau encompassing Kontum, Pleiku, Binh Dinh, and Phu Bon Provinces. It specified the destruction of Special Forces camps at Plei Me, Dak Sut, and Duc Co, the annihilation of the Le Thanh District headquarters, and the seizure of the city of Pleiku. Assault forces included the 32d and 66th North Vietnamese Army Regiments.

By the end of October, following an unsuccessful attempt to capture the Plei Me Special Forces Camp, the 32d and 33d Regiments were being pursued by units of the 1st Cavalry Division's 1st Brigade in the Pleiku area. The American forces had deployed westward from the division base camp at An Khe when the Plei Me Camp was threatened and for twelve days had engaged in intensive search and destroy as well as reconnaissance in force operations, most of them involving fierce fighting and most of them successful.

On 9 November the 1st Brigade was relieved by the 3d, known as the Garry Owen Brigade. This name was a matter of no small pride to the troopers of the 3d Brigade. Originally a Gaelic song once sung by the Irish Lancers, Garry Owen was adopted by the 7th Cavalry Regiment of Lt. Col. George A. Custer during the American Indian wars in the nineteenth century. A mark of the esprit of the 7th Cavalry, the name and new words to the song came to Vietnam with the brigade. The 3d's forces consisted of the 1st and 2d Battalions, 7th Cavalry, joined for this operation by the 2d Battalion, 5th Cavalry.

Concerned that the North Vietnamese might slip away entirely, Maj. Gen. Harry W. O. Kinnard, the 1st Cavalry Division commander, directed Col. Thomas W. Brown, the 3d Brigade commander, to employ his units south and southeast of Plei Me. Colonel Brown, a tall, lean officer, well schooled in airmobile techniques and with plenty of experience in infantry tactics, began on 10 November to press the search vigorously with squad and platoon saturation patrolling.

When three days of patrolling turned up few North Vietnamese, General Kinnard ordered Colonel Brown to search westward toward the Cambodian border. Anxious to engage an enemy that was proving to be more and more elusive, Brown focused his attention on the densely wooded area south of the Ia Drang River at the base of the Chu Pong massif, a rugged mountain mass straddling the South Vietnamese-Cambodian border.

To Brown the prospect of finding the enemy near the banks of the slowly meandering Ia Drang River seemed good. This sector had been a bastion of the Viet Minh who earlier had fought the French in Indochina. And during a recent intelligence briefing Brown had seen on the G-2 situation map, a big red star indicating a probable major base for at least one North Vietnamese regiment, which could be using it as a way station for soldiers infiltrating South Vietnam. Friendly troops, furthermore, had not been in this area for some time. If his efforts failed, Colonel Brown planned to search farther south, even closer to the Cambodian border.

On 10 November General Chu Huy Man, undismayed by his heavy losses in the failure at Plei Me, decided to try again on 16 November. The staging area his headquarters selected in preparation for the new attack included the very terrain Colonel Brown had chosen to search.

The 33d North Vietnamese Army Regiment, originally a 2,200-man fighting force, had lost 890 killed, 100 missing, and 500 wounded during the Plei Me debacle. It now began reorganizing its meagre ranks into a single composite battalion in the valley between the Ia Drang River and Hill 542, the most prominent peak of Chu Pang in this area. Thirteen kilometres westward on the northern bank of the Ia Drang was the 32d North Vietnamese Army Regiment, still a formidable fighting force despite some losses during the recent battle. The force majeure for the second enemy attempt on Plei Me Special Forces Camp was the newly arrived 66th North Vietnamese Army Regiment. By 11 November its three battalions were positioned along both banks of the Ia Drang, a few kilometers west of the 33d Regiment. Although General Chu Huy Man intended to reinforce the three regiments with a battalion each of 120-mm. mortars and 14.5-mm. twin-barrel antiaircraft guns, both units were still on the Ho Chi Minh Trail in Cambodia, en route to the staging area.

Colonel Brown's plan, meanwhile, was developing. On 13 November he directed his operations officer, Maj. Henri-Gerard ("Pete") Mallet, who until a few weeks before had been the 2d Battalion, 7th Cavalry, executive officer, to move the 1st Battalion, 7th Cavalry, to a new area of operations southwest of Plei Me and to prepare a fragmentary order that would put the battalion at the base of the Chu Pong peak (Hill 542) as a jump-off point for search and destroy operations in the vicinity.

On the same day Major Mallet, grease pencil in hand, outlined an area comprising roughly fifteen square kilometers on the situation map. Heretofore the search areas assigned to the infantry battalions had been color-designated. Having run out of primary colors at this point, he designated the sector, which was shaped like an artist's pallet, Area LIME.

At 1700 on the 13th Colonel Brown was with Lt. Col. Harold G. Moore, Jr., the 1st Battalion, 7th Cavalry, commander, at his Company A command post south of Plei Me. He told Moore to execute an airmobile assault into the Ia Drang valley north of the Chu Pong peak early the next morning and to conduct search and destroy operations through 15 November. Although the brigade had been allocated 24 helicopters a day, Colonel Brown could provide the 1st Battalion, 7th Cavalry, with only 16 for the move because his other two battalions needed 4 each for resupply purposes and some local movement of elements of squad and platoon size. Fire support, so important to an air assault, was to be provided by two 105-mm. howitzer batteries of the 1st Battalion, 21st Artillery. They would be firing from Landing Zone Falcon nine kilometers east of the search area. One battery was to be airlifted from Plei Me to Falcon early on the 14th before the assault; the other was already in position. A note of concern in his voice, Colonel Brown reminded Moore to keep his rifle companies within supporting range of each other. Both men were sharply conscious that the battalion had yet to be tested in battle against a large enemy force.

Colonel Moore returned to his command post at Plei Me, where his headquarters soon buzzed with activity. Radioing his Company A and Company C commanders, whose troops were engaged in saturation patrolling throughout their sectors, the tall Kentuckian told them to concentrate their men at first light on 14 November at the largest pickup zones in each sector and to be ready themselves to take a look at the target area. He arranged for the helicopters to lift Company B back to Plei Me early on the morning of the 14th from brigade headquarters, twenty minutes away to the southwest. The unit had just been placed there on the evening of the 13th to secure Colonel Brown's command post and other administrative and logistical facilities. Setting 0830 the following morning as the time for issuing the order, which would be preceded by a reconnaissance flight, Moore continued supervising preparations until by 2200 everything had been accomplished that could be done before the aerial reconnaissance.

That night before going to bed Colonel Moore reviewed his plan and decided on a fresh approach for this operation. Instead of setting down each company on a separate landing zone as he had been doing for the past few days, he would use one landing zone for the entire battalion. His whole force would then be available if he encountered the enemy on landing. Although American units had not engaged a sizable enemy force for some time, the big red star designating a possible enemy base that both he and Colonel Brown had seen on the map loomed large in his mind.

Colonel Moore considered his assets. Firepower would be no problem. The 21st Artillery, tactical air, and gunships had given him excellent support in previous operations, and he knew that Colonel Brown would provide additional fire support if he needed it.

The manpower situation was somewhat different. Of the twenty-three officers authorized for his three rifle companies and one combat support company, twenty were available and practically all had been with the

Major Bruce P. Crandall, 1965

battalion since air assault testing days at Fort Benning, Georgia. In the enlisted ranks the scene was less encouraging, for the 1st Battalion, 7th Cavalry, would be at only two-thirds strength. During the unit's first two months in Vietnam, malaria and individual service terminations had taken their toll. At the moment, 8 to 10 men from the battalion were in transit for rest and recuperation, and each company had kept 3 to 5 men each back at Camp Radcliff, the An Khe permanent base camp, for various reasons—minor illness, guard duty, administrative retention, base camp development. Colonel Moore was not unduly concerned, however, for he had accomplished previous search and destroy missions with approximately the same numbers. Besides, rarely did any commander field a unit at 100 percent strength.

The 14th dawned bright and clear and by 0630 Company B had been lifted to Plei Me from brigade headquarters by CH-47 Chinook helicopters. Since it had already been assembled in one location,

Colonel Moore had selected Company B to land first.

While he supervised preparations, Capt. John D. Herren, Company B commander, chewed on his pipe and thought of the impending operation. He and his men had gone without sleep the night before, having had to cope with an understandably jittery brigade command post. A few minutes before midnight on the 12th the post had been attacked by a local Viet Cong force that killed seven men and wounded twenty-three. Herren could only trust that the lack of rest would have little effect on the fighting ability of his men.

Amid a deafening roar of helicopters, the reconnaissance party assembled. The ships, finished with Herren's company, had begun to move Battery A, 1st Battalion, 21st Artillery, to Falcon, where it would join Battery C as planned. Standing there to hear Colonel Moore were the Company B, Company D, and headquarters company commanders; a scout section leader from Troop C, 1st Squadron, 9th Cavalry; the commander of Company A, 229th Aviation Battalion (Airmobile), Maj. Bruce P. Crandall; and the battalion S-3, Capt. Gregory P. Dillon. Moore briefed the group on the battalion's mission, the flight route, and what to look for. Then, using two UH-1D Huey helicopters and escorted by two UH-1D gunships, the reconnaissance party departed.

Flying at 2,500 feet and following a pattern that would both provide some deception and allow for maximum viewing of the target area, the four helicopters headed southwest to a point about eight kilometers southeast of the Ia Drang River. Then they turned and flew due north to Duc Co where they circled for five minutes, reversed course, and by 0815 returned to Plei Me. (Map 2)

Once on the ground, the members of the party discussed possible landing zones to be chosen from open areas observed during the flight. While they were debating, the brigade fragmentary order, which specified Area LIME as the primary zone of interest, arrived. Within a few minutes the choice narrowed to three landing zones: TANGO, X-RAY, and YANKEE. Colonel Moore wanted the largest site available, one that would not unduly restrict the helicopters. This ruled out TANGO as inadequate. Surrounded by tall trees, it could accommodate three, perhaps four, Hueys at most, or half a rifle platoon. Both YANKEE and X-RAY seemed likely choices, for either could take eight to ten ships at a time; at lead a platoon and a half could be put

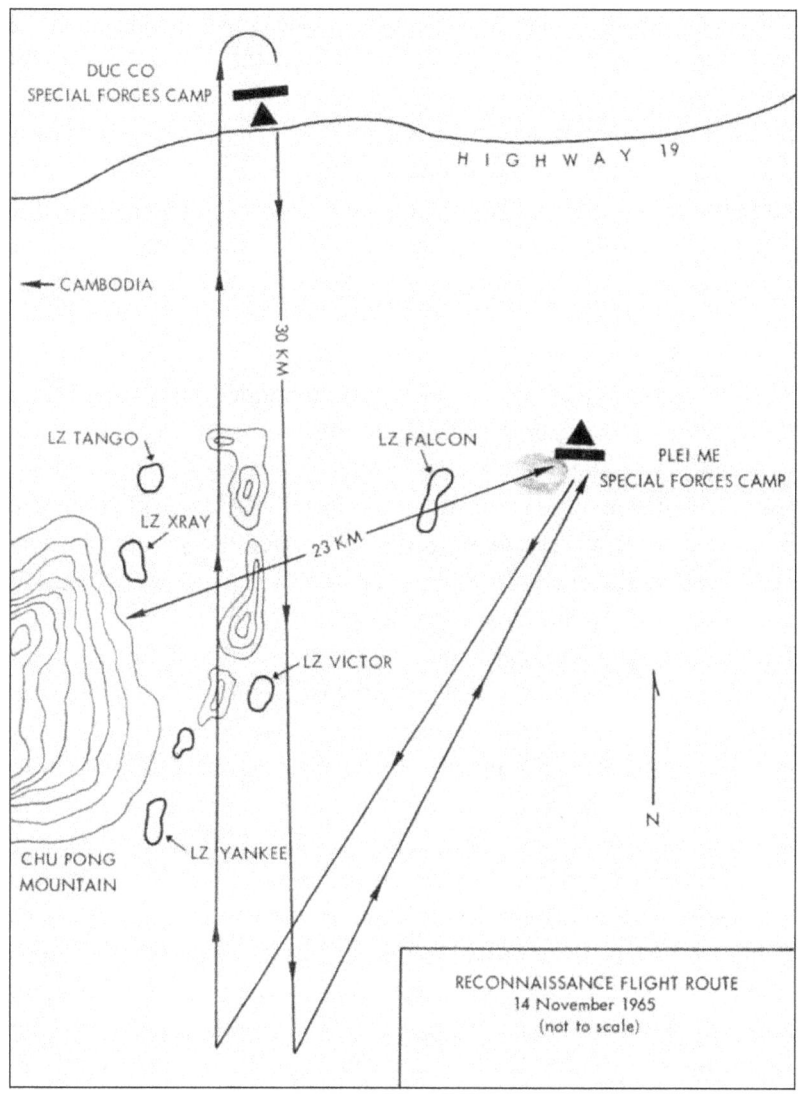

Map 2. Reconnaissance flight route, 14 November 1965

on the ground at the start, that most crucial of all moments during an airmobile assault. Announcing X-RAY as his tentative choice, Colonel Moore turned to the scout section leader from the 9th Cavalry and instructed him to fly another reconnaissance mission at "nap-of-the-earth" level along the Ia Drang valley. He was to obtain more details about X-RAY, YANKEE, and the surrounding terrain and to look for any signs of enemy activity.

The scout section was back in forty minutes. Although the pilots had seen several trails during their low-level flight, they had drawn no enemy fire. YANKEE, they reported, was usable but risky because it had too many high tree stumps. X-RAY, they confirmed, could easily take eight to ten ships, and just a few hundred meters north of it they had seen communications wire stretched along an east-west trail. This last bit of intelligence was all Colonel Moore needed. X-RAY was to be the primary site, with YANKEE and TANGO as alternates to be used only on his order.

By this time it was 0855 and with the planning completed Colonel Moore reassembled the company commanders, his staff, and representatives of supporting forces to hear his order.

According to the latest available intelligence, an enemy battalion was located five kilometers northwest of X-RAY. Another hostile force of undetermined size was probably just southwest of the landing zone itself, and a secret base was believed to be three kilometers to the northwest. To develop these targets, Moore explained, the 1st Battalion was going to make an air assault into X-RAY, then search for and destroy enemy forces, concentrating on stream beds and wooded high ground. The low-level reconnaissance had no doubt alerted any enemy in the area. To keep the enemy guessing up to the last as to where an actual landing would occur, the 21st Artillery was to fire an 8-minute diversionary preparation on YANKEE and TANGO. This was to be followed by a 20-minute rain of fire on X-RAY, with emphasis on the slopes of a finger with a contiguous draw that jutted out from Chu Pang just northwest of X-RAY. Gunships of the 2d Battalion, 20th Artillery (Aerial Rocket) (Airmobile), were to follow the tube artillery barrage for thirty seconds with rocket and machine gun fire, after which the escort gunships of Company A, 229th Aviation Battalion, were to sweep the area.

Using sixteen Hueys, Herren's Company B was to follow close on the heels of the fire preparation, land, and secure X-RAY, followed in turn and on order by Companies A, C, and D. Once on the ground Companies A and B were to assemble in attack formation just off the north and northeastern sectors of X-RAY, prepared to search east or northeast on order, with Company A on the right. Designated at first as the reserve force, Company C was upon landing to assume the security mission from Company B on order with a "be prepared"

Transport helicopters landing infantrymen

task tot move west and northwest, searching the lower portion of Chu Pong. If Company C did hit anything, Moore reasoned, at least he would have his entire force readily available as a backup. Company B had priority of fire at the start, but once the westward push from X-RAY began the priority was shifted to Company A.

Colonel Moore directed each rifle company to bring one 81-mm. mortar tube and a maximum ammunition load and Company D to bring its three tubes. When all companies had closed at X-RAY, their mortars were to revert to control of the Company D mortar platoon.

Just as he completed his briefing, Colonel Moore learned that the artillery was in position. Setting 1030 as touchdown time at X-RAY for the air assault, with the 20-minute artillery preparatory fires to be completed by H minus 1 minute, Moore knew that it would be a split-second affair.

For this mission the troops of the 1st Battalion, 7th Cavalry, would be well prepared. Standing operating procedure dictated that each rifleman carry at least 300 rounds of M16 ammunition, and each grenadier was ordered to bring between two and three dozen high-explosive shells for his 40-mm. grenade launcher. Machine gun crews were to transport at least 800 rounds of linked 7.62-mm. ammunition, and every man was to have no less than two M26 fragmentation grenades. There were to be at least two 66-mm M72 light assault weapons per squad and five to six smoke grenades in each platoon. Every soldier was to carry one C ration meal and two canteens of water, as well as an ample supply of entrenching tools and machetes.

Colonel Brown arrived as Moore finished giving the order and Moore briefed him separately. The brigade commander liked the tactical plan, agreed with the selection of X-RAY as the primary landing zone, and was satisfied that Moore's concept of the operation followed the guidance he had given him the previous afternoon.

At 1017, after a brief delay resulting from the too hasty positioning of the artillery pieces at FALCON, the preparatory fires began. Thirteen minutes later the leading elements of Company B lifted off the Plei Me airstrip with a thunderous roar in a storm of red dust. With volleys of artillery fire slamming into the objective area, the sixteen Hueys—four platoons of four each—filed southwestward across the midmorning sky at two thousand feet. Two kilometers out, they dropped to treetop level. The aerial rocket artillery gunships meanwhile worked X RAY over for thirty seconds, expending half of their loads, then circled nearby, available on call. The 229th's escort gunships came next, rockets and machine guns blazing, immediately ahead of the lift ships. As the lead helicopters braked for the assault landing, their door gunners and some of the infantrymen fired into the trees and tall grass.

Lunging from the ships, the men of Company B, Colonel Moore among them, charged into the trees, snap-firing at likely enemy positions. By 1048 the helicopters were already returning to Plei Me for the rest of Company B and advance contingents of Company A.

Relatively flat and open as seen from above, X-RAY took on a different appearance when viewed by the infantryman on the ground. Ringed by sparse scrub brush with occasional trees ranging upward to a hundred feet, the landing zone was covered with hazel-colored, willowy elephant grass as high as five feet, ideal for the concealment of crawling soldiers. Interspersed throughout were anthills, some considerably taller than a standing man, all excellent as crew-served weapons positions. Along the western and northeastern edges of the landing zone the trees were especially thick and extended up the slopes of Chu Pong peak, which was 542 meters high and whose thick vegetation offered good concealment for enemy troops. A dry creek bed with waist-high banks ran along the western edge of the landing zone.

Captain Herren watched with satisfaction as his 1st Platoon leader, 2d Lt. Alan E. Deveny, went about the business of securing the landing zone. In line with orders from Colonel Moore, Herren was using a new technique. Rather than attempt a 360-degree perimeter coverage of the entire area as in previous operations, Herren concealed most of his force in a clump of trees and tall grass near the center of the landing zone as a reaction striking force, while Deveny's squads struck out in different directions, reconnoitering the terrain fifty to a hundred meters from the western side of X-RAY. A sound technique, it allowed Captain Herren to conserve his forces while he retained a flexible option, which, in view of the 30-minute turnaround flight time for the rest of the battalion, appeared prudent.

As Lieutenant Deveny's soldiers pressed the search, Herren became fully convinced that if there was to be a fight the proximity of X-RAY to the enemy haven across the Cambodian border made X-RAY the likely site. Yet the leading elements of the 1st Battalion, 7th Cavalry, had landed successfully and were thus far unopposed.

Where was the enemy?

The helicopter landing had been spotted. Although elements of the North Vietnamese units that had been scheduled to participate in the 16 November Plei Me attack had left their Ia Drang valley staging areas at dawn the morning of 14 November, the landing of Captain Herren's infantrymen in X-RAY a few hours later had prompted General Chu Huy Man to change course swiftly. Plei Me would have to wait. The 66th and 33d Regiments would attack the landing zone and destroy the Americans. By noon two battalions of the 66th and the newly formed composite battalion of the 33d were preparing for the assault from positions at the base of Chu Pong and the low ground immediately to the west.

At X-RAY the 1st Platoon, Company B, continued to probe. At 1120 Lieutenant Deveny's troops made a discovery: searching the brush, a rifleman surprised an enemy soldier only fifty meters from the landing zone. The North Vietnamese tried to lose himself in the thicket, but the Americans soon captured him. He was unarmed, dressed in trousers and a dirty khaki shirt with a serial number on one of the epaulets, and carried only an empty canteen.

Notified of the catch, Colonel Moore rushed to the spot with his intelligence officer, Capt. Thomas C. Metsker, and his Montagnard interpreter, a Mr. Nik. Questioning the prisoner, they learned that he was a deserter from the North Vietnamese Army and had been subsisting on bananas for five days. He declared that three North Vietnamese battalions were on Chu Pong mountain, anxious to kill Americans but as yet unable to find them.

Elated but cautious, for getting the rest of the battalion in quickly and safely was now doubly important, Colonel Moore told Captain Herren to intensify his search and prepare to assume Company C's mission of exploring the terrain at the foot of Chu Pong, giving special attention to the finger and draw to the northwest. Moore radioed his S-3, Captain Dillon, who was circling the landing zone in the command helicopter, to land and pick up the prisoner and fly him back to 3d Brigade headquarters for additional interrogation.

Hardly had Moore given Herren his mission when the commander of Company A, Capt. Ramon A. Nadal II, reported. A former Special Forces officer on a second Vietnam tour, Nadal begged permission for his company to follow the lead opened up by Company B's find. Moore had already given the job to Herren, whose men now knew the terrain and were tensed for an approaching fight; he told Nadal to assume the mission of providing security for the landing zone.

For the move northwest Captain Herren directed Lieutenant Deveny's 1st Platoon toward the finger, with 2d Lt. Henry T. Herrick's 2d Platoon on the right. He told both officers to advance abreast. Positioning 2d Lt. Dennis J. Deal's 3d Platoon behind the 1st as a reserve, Captain Herren and his company moved out.

Deveny got ahead of Herrick's platoon after crossing the dry creek bed which ran along the eastern flank of the finger. At 1245 his platoon encountered an enemy force of about platoon size which attacked both his flanks with small arms fire. Pinned down and suffering casualties, he asked for help. Captain Herren, in an attempt to relieve the pressure, radioed Lieutenant Herrick to establish contact with the 1st Platoon's right flank.

Anxious to develop the situation, Herrick manoeuvred his 27-man force in that direction. A few minutes after Herren issued the order, the point of Herrick's 2d Platoon bumped into a squad of North Vietnamese soldiers moving toward X-RAY along a well-used trail, parallel to the platoon's direction of advance. The startled enemy turned and scurried back along the trail; firing, the 2d Platoon followed in close pursuit, with two squads forward. The platoon soon began to receive sporadic but ineffective enfilade fire from the right. The lead squads were now at the crest of the finger, about a hundred meters from the dry creek bed. To the right and farther downhill was the 3d Squad.

Lieutenant Herrick intended to continue his sweep, with all three squads on the line and machine guns on the flanks. Although he could no longer see the enemy soldiers, he knew that they were somewhere in front of him. He was about to give the signal to continue when men in his 3d Squad spotted about twenty North Vietnamese scrambling toward two large anthills off the platoon's left flank. As the last of the enemy disappeared behind the anthills, the 3d Squad opened fire. The North Vietnamese returned it, but a 3d Squad grenadier found the range and in less than a minute was pumping round after round into their ranks. Screams mingled with the sound of the explosions. Without warning, a blistering volley of enemy fire suddenly erupted from the right flank. The opening fusillade killed the grenadier and pinned down the rest of the squad.

Deploying his two M60 machine guns toward the harassed force, Herrick yelled to the 3d Squad leader, S. Sgt. Clyde E. Savage, to pull back under covering fire of the machine guns. Yet even as the gunners moved into firing position and Herrick radioed word of his predicament to his company commander, the situation grew worse. Within a few minutes fire was lashing the entire 3d Platoon from all sides. Covered by the blazing M60's, Sergeant Savage managed to withdraw his squad toward the platoon, carrying the M79 of the dead grenadier, who lay sprawled where he had fallen, a .45caliber pistol clutched in his right hand. Amid increasingly heavy fire of all calibers, including mortars and rockets, the squad reached the main body of the platoon and joined the other men in hastily forming a 25-meter perimeter.

The machine gunners were less fortunate in making their way into the perimeter. Although the closer team managed to disengage and crawl into the small circle of prone infantrymen, enemy fire cut down all four in the other team. Seizing the fallen team's M60, the North Vietnamese turned it against Herrick's positions.

Except for the artillery forward observer, 1st Lt. William O. Riddle, who soon caught up with Lieutenant Deal, Captain Herren and his command group had dropped behind the leading platoons while Herren radioed a situation report to Colonel Moore. To the Company B commander, who could hear the firelight going on in the jungle ahead, the enemy appeared to be in two-company strength and fully capable of cutting off Lieutenant Herrick's 2d Platoon. Yet Captain Herren had few resources to turn to Herrick's assistance. Already he had committed his 3d Platoon to go to the aid of Lieutenant Deveny, and the company's lone 81-mm. mortar was in action, making quick work of the meager forty rounds of high-explosive ammunition the crew had brought to the landing zone.

Since Deveny appeared to be less closely engaged than Herrick, Captain Herren ordered him to try to reach Herrick. If Deal's force could reach Deveny soon enough, together they stood a good chance of reaching Herrick.

Having reported the action to Colonel Moore, Captain Herren turned from his radio just in time to see a North Vietnamese soldier not more than fifteen meters away with a weapon trained on him. Rapidly, Herren fired a burst from his M16, ducked for cover, and tossed a grenade.

Off to his left, Herren could just make out men crouched in the dry stream bed, firing toward the finger. Believing them to be members of his 3d Platoon and anxious to get them linked up with his 1st Platoon, he headed toward them.

At the landing zone Colonel Moore had meanwhile alerted Captain Nadal to be prepared to assist Herren as soon as Company C was on the ground. The heavy firelight had barely commenced when Company A's last platoon and the dead forces of Company C landed. It was 1330. A few rounds of enemy 60-mm. and 81-mm. mortar fire slammed into the tall elephant grass in the center of the landing zone as Colonel Moore turned to Nadal and ordered him to rush a platoon to Herren to be used in getting through to Herrick. Captain Nadal was to follow with his remaining two platoons and link up with Company B's left flank. Colonel Moore then turned to Capt. Robert H. Edwards, who had just landed with some of his troops, and directed him to set up a blocking position to the south and southwest of X-RAY, just inside the tree line, where he could cover Company A's exposed left flank. Moore knew that this was a risky move because he had only Company D left as a reaction force and still had to defend an entire landing zone in all directions. By this positioning of Edwards' company he would be exposing his rear, but in the light of the rapidly developing situation, which bore out what the prisoner had told him, it seemed the only sensible thing to do.

The S-3, Captain Dillon, had by now returned from brigade headquarters and was hovering above X-RAY, relaying the course of the battle to Colonel Brown's headquarters.

Colonel Moore had established his command post near a prominent anthill in the center of the landing zone. He radioed Dillon to request air strikes, artillery, and aerial rocket fire, starting on the lower fringes of the Chu Pong slopes and then working first over the western and then over the southern enemy approaches to X-RAY. Secondary targets would be the draws leading down from the mountain and any suspected or sighted enemy mortar positions. Priority was to be given to requests for fire fro m the fighting companies.

Dillon passed the fire requests to Capt. Jerry E. Whiteside, the 21st. Artillery liaison officer, and Lt. Charles Hastings, the Air Force forward air controller, who were seated beside him. A few minutes later, Pleiku-based aircraft were blasting the target area, and two strikes were made on the valley floor to the northwest, near the suspected location of the enemy battalion.

Although the artillery also responded quickly, the fire was at first ineffective. Since there were no well-defined terrain features that could be used as reference points to the fighting troops, now hidden by a heavy pall of dust and smoke that hung in the air, it was hard to pinpoint locations for close-in support. Aware of the difficulty, Colonel Moore radioed Whiteside to use the technique of "walking" the fires down the mountain toward the landing zone from the south and the west, and fires were soon close enough to aid some of the embattled infantrymen.

Anxious to assist Company B, Captain Nadal radioed his 2d Platoon leader, 2d Lt. Walter J. Marm, to move forward. Marm formed his platoon into a skirmish line and started out immediately from the landing zone toward the sound of the firing. Since there was no time to consult with Captain Herren, Lieutenant Marm planned to join the Company B left flank and push through to Lieutenant Herrick's perimeter. No sooner had he crossed the dry creek bed when two

Men of the 1st Cavalry Division (airmobile) in action during the battle of Ia Drang

North Vietnamese appeared before his platoon and surrendered. A few moments later, just as he reached Deal's 3d Platoon, troops of both units spotted a force of khaki-clad enemy soldiers moving across their front, left to right. Both Deal and Marm had apparently met the left enveloping pincer which had initially flanked Herrick and which was now attempting, it seemed, to surround all of Company B. A fierce firefight ensued, both sides taking casualties. The enemy soldiers then peeled off to the left, breaking contact momentarily and, unknown to Marm, trying to maneuver behind Marm via the dry creek bed.

Taking advantage of the lull, Marm collected all of his and Deal's wounded and ordered one of his squad leaders, S. Sgt. Lonnie L. Parker, to take them back to the landing zone. Parker tried but returned in twenty minutes to report that the platoon was surrounded. Marm doubted that the enemy could have moved that fast but he could not be sure, since enemy troops were now maneuvering to his flank also.

When the North Vietnamese of the flanking force, estimated as company size, entered the dry creak bed they ran headlong into the rest of Company A; Nadal, eager to join the fray, had moved his remaining two platoons forward. First to meet the enemy in the creek bed was the 3d Platoon. The firing was at very close range, the fighting savage. The platoon leader, 2d Lt. Robert E. Taft going to the aid of one of his squad leaders who, unknown to Taft, was already dead, was himself hit in the throat and died instantly. Recoiling from the first shock, the men of the left half of the 3d Platoon climbed onto the creak bank where, along with the men of the 1st Platoon, they poured a murderous fire into the enemy. A seriously wounded rifleman lay near the body of Lieutenant Taft beneath the deadly cross fire.

As the firelight erupted in the dry creak bed, additional elements of Company C and the lead troopers of Company D landed at X-RAY in the first eight Hueys of the fifth airlift. They touched down in a heavy hail of enemy small arms fire that wounded a pilot and a door gunner.

Capt. Louis R. LeFebvre, the Company D commander, in the lead helicopter, could see the air strikes and artillery fire slamming into the ground around X-RAY. Leaning forward to unhook his seat belt as the aircraft touched down, he felt a bullet crease the back of his neck. Instinctively, he turned to the right just in time to see his radio operator slump forward, still buckled in his seat, a bullet hole in the left side of his head. Grabbing the dead man's radio, LeFebvre jumped from the helicopter, told those assembled who had landed in other ships to follow, and raced for the tree line to the west, seventy-five meters away. Only four men followed him. Under fire all the way, they reached the relative safety of the dry creek bed, thirty-five meters short of the tree line.

So heavy was the fire, particularly in the northwestern area, that Colonel Moore radioed the remaining eight helicopters not to land. Sporadic rocket and mortar fire, the crash of artillery volleys, and the thunderclap of air strikes that were now ringing the small clearing blended in one continuous roar.

Captain LeFebvre heard firing in front of him and on both sides. His small group had moved into position just to the right of Company A's two platoons, which were still battling the force that had attempted to flank Marm's platoon. LeFebvre and his men joined the firing from their positions in the creek bed, their immediate targets twenty-five to thirty North Vietnamese moving to the left across their front. Soon realizing the need for more firepower, LeFebvre called for his antitank platoon (which had been reorganized into a rifle platoon) to join him. It had come in with him on the last flight and was 150 meters to his rear, assembled on the landing zone, awaiting instructions. The acting platoon leader, S. Sgt. George Gonzales answered that he was on the way. LeFebvre then yelled to his mortar platoon leader, 1st Lt. Raul E. Requera Taboada, who had accompanied him in the lead ship and lay a few feet away from him, to send his radio operator forward to replace the man who had been killed in the helicopter.

Just as the radio operator joined him, Captain LeFebvre looked up to see Captain Herren. The Company B commander told him that there were enemy soldiers south in the direction from which he had come. He and his radio operator took positions beside LeFebvre and began firing along with the others. In rapid succession, Herren's radio operator was killed, LeFebvre's right arm was shattered by a fusillade of enemy small arms fire, and Taboada received a bad leg wound. Herren applied a tourniquet to LeFebvre's arm and then resumed firing.

With half of the fifth lift landed, Company C had all of its troops except three Huey loads. While the Company A firefight raged, Captain Edwards, in accordance with Colonel Moore's guidance, quickly moved his platoons into a blocking position, occupying 120 meters of ground immediately adjacent to Nadal's right flank. Edwards was none too soon. A few minutes later a strong enemy force struck Company C from the southwest and west. Lying prone, the Americans put out a withering volley of fire. The North Vietnamese soldiers, estimated at a reinforced company, wore helmets and web equipment and, like those who had hit Companies A and B, were well camouflaged. With the help of well-placed air strikes and artillery fire, however, Company C held them off, killing many. The 1st Platoon managed to capture a prisoner, who was quickly evacuated.

Colonel Moore's gamble in positioning Edwards' forces south of Nadal's rather than to the north proved sound, for by the timely commitment of Companies A and C he had so far succeeded in frustrating enemy attempts to overrun the landing zone. But with his rear still exposed, he directed Edwards to tie in and co-ordinate with Company D to his left, extending the perimeter south and southeast into the brush.

Edwards found Sergeant Gonzales, who had assumed command of Company D after Captain LeFebvre had been evacuated. Leaving skeleton crews to man the mortars, together they quickly moved the antitank platoon and some of the mortar platoon alongside Company

C. The reconnaissance platoon had not yet arrived.

While co-ordinating with Gonzales, Captain Edwards learned that the mortars had not been centrally organized. With Colonel Moore's approval, Edwards placed them under his own section leader's control until the battalion mortar platoon leader should arrive with his fire direction center. But the mortars were unable to provide effective fire support because smoke, noise, and confusion made it difficult for the forward observers to adjust. The intensity of the fighting increased as did the noise. Hit by heavy enemy ground fire while making a low-level firing pass over X-RAY, an A-1E Skyraider, trailing smoke and flames, crashed two kilometers northeast of the landing zone, killing the pilot. When enemy soldiers tried to reach the wreckage, helicopter gunships destroyed it with rocket fire.

By this time it was a few minutes before 1500 and, judging by reports from his companies, Colonel Moore estimated that a North Vietnamese force numbering at least 500 to 600 opposed his battalion, with more on the way. Calling Colonel Brown, he asked for another rifle company.

At brigade headquarters, Colonel Brown was following developments closely. Monitoring the 1st Battalion, 7th Cavalry, tactical situation by radio, he had realized from the report of Company B's contact and what followed that the battalion was going to have its hands full. By 1430 he was in the air above X-RAY to see the situation for himself. Below him as the battle raged, he noticed that the artillery was firing halfway up Chu Pong. He radioed Colonel Moore to bring it in closer where it could be more effective. He did not know that Colonel Moore had arranged for the artillery to fire farther out at secondary target areas when not shooting specific close-in missions.

Convinced of the seriousness of the situation, Colonel Brown had given careful consideration to what action to take if Colonel Moore asked for help. Of his two other battalions only one company was assembled at one place—Company B, 2d Battalion, 7th Cavalry, whose troops had just begun to arrive at brigade headquarters for perimeter security duty. These troops were, therefore, the logical choice, and when Moore called for assistance Colonel Brown in mid-afternoon attached Company B to the 1st Battalion, 7th Cavalry. Another company replaced the troops as perimeter guard at brigade headquarters.

It seemed obvious to Colonel Brown as the afternoon wore on that the enemy was trying to annihilate the 1st Battalion, 7th Cavalry. Looking to the future, he prepared for further reinforcements. Shortly after approving the use of Company B, 2d Battalion, 7th Cavalry, Colonel Brown called Lt. Col. Robert B. Tully, who commanded the 2d Battalion, 5th Cavalry, and directed him to assemble his unit as quickly as possible at Landing Zone VICTOR, which lay three kilometers to the southeast. Since he did not relish the idea of moving a steady stream of helicopters into what might still be a hot landing zone, and since he felt certain that the enemy would expect such a maneuver and would probably be prepared to deal with it, Brown told Tully that he would move by foot to reinforce Moore's battalion at X-RAY the next morning. He then directed the remainder of the 2d Battalion, 7th Cavalry, to move to Landing Zone MACON, a few kilometers north of X-RAY, where it would be closer to the fight and available if needed.

By 1500 Colonel Moore had decided that it was absolutely essential, and safe enough, for the remaining tactical elements of the 2d Battalion to land. Although the eastern sector of the perimeter was still under enemy fire, the fire had slackened considerably because of the actions of Company C and Company D. In minutes after receiving the landing order, the battalion reconnaissance platoon, Company C's three loads of troops, and the executive officer and the first sergeant of Company D were on the ground. Colonel Moore directed 2d Lt. James L. Litton, the executive officer, to take over from Sergeant Gonzales, who had been wounded, coordinate all mortars in the battalion under one central fire direction center, and deploy the reconnaissance platoon around the northeastern fringe of the landing zone as a battalion reserve and to provide security in the area.

Although by this time Colonel Moore, in an attempt to minimize the ships' exposure to enemy fire, was personally directing the helicopter traffic into X-RAY, two helicopters were disabled during the landing. One received enemy fire in the engine compartment while lifting off and had to make a forced landing in an open area just off the northern edge of X-RAY. Another clipped the treetops with the main rotor blade when landing and could not be flown out. Both crews, who were uninjured, were evacuated almost immediately while the helicopters, secured by Company D troopers, awaited lift-out later.

Combat operations at Ia Drang in November 1965. Major Crandall's UH-1 Huey dispatches infantry while under fire.

Other helicopter crews nevertheless continued to fly missions into X-RAY, exhibiting great courage and audacity under fire.

On the ground, the welfare of men who were wounded was considerably improved by the fact that four aidmen and the battalion surgeon had landed with medical supplies early in the afternoon. They had set up an emergency aid station near Moore's command post. Rather than expose medical evacuation helicopters to enemy fire, Colonel Moore arranged with the helicopter lift company commander, Major Crandall, to evacuate casualties to FALCON by loading them on departing lift ships. With the help of a pathfinder team which arrived by 1600, the system worked well.

Within a half hour after the rest of the battalion had closed into X-RAY, the forces of Company A and Company B that had been attempting to reach Lieutenant Herrick's platoon pulled back to the dry creek bed under covering artillery and mortar fire at Colonel Moore's direction, bringing their dead and wounded along. Although Company B's 1st Platoon (with 2d Lt. Kenneth E. Duncan, the company executive officer, overseeing the operation) had advanced to a point within seventy-five meters of the isolated force and had eventually linked up with the 3d Platoon, all attempts to reach Herrick had been unsuccessful. The 1st Battalion, 7th Cavalry, clearly was facing an aggressive, expertly camouflaged, and well-armed enemy force that could shoot well and was not afraid to die. Nevertheless, Colonel Moore decided to give it another try. He ordered Companies A and B to prepare for a coordinated attack, supported by heavy preparatory fires, to reach the beleaguered platoon, while Companies C and D, the former still engaged in a violent fight, continued to hold the line on the perimeter.

The predicament of the isolated force meanwhile grew progressively worse. Lieutenant Herrick and his men sorely needed the reinforcements that Colonel Moore was attempting to send. The North Vietnamese laced the small perimeter with fire so low to the ground that few of Herrick's men were able to employ their intrenching tools to provide themselves cover. Through it all the men returned the fire, taking a heavy toll of the enemy. Sergeant Savage, firing his M16, hit twelve of the enemy himself during the course of the afternoon. In mid afternoon Lieutenant Herrick was hit by a bullet which entered his hip, coursed through his body, and went out through his right shoulder. As he lay dying, the lieutenant continued to direct his perimeter defense, and in his last few moments he gave his signal operation instructions book to S. Sgt. Carl L. Palmer, his platoon sergeant, with orders to burn it if capture seemed imminent. He told Palmer to redistribute the ammunition, call in artillery fire, and at the first opportunity try to make a break for it. Sergeant Palmer, himself already slightly wounded had no sooner taken command than he too was killed.

The 2d Squad leader took charge. He rose on his hands and knees and mumbled to no one in particular that he was going to get the platoon out of danger. He had just finished the sentence when a bullet smashed into his head. Killed in the same hail of bullets was the forward observer for the 81-mm. mortar. The artillery reconnaissance sergeant, who had been travelling with the platoon, was shot in the neck. Seriously wounded, he became delirious and the men had difficulty keeping him quiet.

Sergeant Savage, the 3d Squad leader, now took command. Snatching the artilleryman's radio, he began calling in and adjusting artillery fire. Within minutes he had ringed the perimeter with well-placed concentrations, some as close to the position as twenty meters. The fire did much to discourage attempts to overrun the perimeter, but the platoon's position still was precarious. Of the 27 men in the platoon, 8 had been killed and 12 wounded, leaving less than a squad of effectives.

After the first unsuccessful attempt to rescue the isolated force, Company B's two remaining platoons had returned to the creek bed where they met Captain Herren. Lieutenants Deveny and Deal listened intently as their company commander explained that an artillery preparation would precede the two-company assault that Colonel Moore planned. Lieutenant Riddle, the company's artillery forward observer, would direct the fire. The platoons would then advance abreast from the dry creek bed.

The creek bed was also to serve as a line of departure for Captain Nadal's company. The Company A soldiers removed their packs and received an ammunition resupply in preparation for the move. Aside from the danger directly in front of him, Nadal believed the greatest threat would come from the left, toward Chu Pong, and accordingly he planned to advance with his company echeloned in that direction, the 2d Platoon leading, followed by the 1st and 3d in that order. Since he was unsure of the trapped platoon's location, Captain Nadal decided to guide on Company B. If he met no significant resistance after travelling a short distance, he would shift to a company wedge formation. Before embarking on his formidable task, Nadal assembled as many of his men as possible in the creek bed and told them that an American platoon was cut off, in trouble, and that they were going after it. The men responded enthusiastically.

Preceded by heavy artillery and aerial rocket fire, most of which fell as close as 250 meters in front of Company B, which had fire priority, the attack to reach the cutoff platoon struck out at 1620, Companies A and B abreast. Almost from the start it was rough going. So close to the creek bed had the enemy infiltrated that heavy fighting broke out almost as soon as the men left it. Well camouflaged, their khaki uniforms blending in with the brownish-yellow elephant grass, the North Vietnamese soldiers had also concealed themselves in trees, burrowed into the ground to make "spider" holes, and dug into the tops and sides of anthills.

The first man in his company out of the creek bed, Captain Nadal had led his 1st and 2d Platoons only a short distance before they encountered the enemy. The 3d Platoon had not yet left the creek bed.

2d Lt. Wayne O. Johnson fell, seriously wounded, and a few moments later a squad leader yelled that one of his team leaders had been killed.

Lieutenant Marm's men forged ahead until enemy machine gun fire, which seemed to come from an anthill thirty meters to their front, stopped them. Deliberately exposing himself in order to pinpoint the exact enemy location, Marm fired an M72 antitank round at the earth mound. He inflicted some casualties, but the enemy fire still continued. Figuring that it would be a simple matter to dash up to the position and toss a grenade behind it, he motioned to one of his men to do so. At this point the noise and confusion was such that a sergeant near him interpreted the gesture as a command to throw one from his position. He tossed and the grenade fell short. Disregarding his own safety, Marm dashed quickly across the open stretch of ground and hurled the grenade into the position, killing some of the enemy soldiers behind it and finishing off the dazed survivors with his M16. Soon afterward he took a bullet in the face and had to be evacuated. (For this action he received the Medal of Honor.)

Captain Nadal watched the casualties mount as his men attempted to inch forward. All of his platoon leaders were dead or wounded and his artillery forward observer had been killed. Four of his men were killed within six feet of him, including Sfc. Jacke Gell, his communications sergeant, who had been filling in as a radio operator. It was a little past 1700 and soon it would be dark. Nadal's platoons had moved only 150 meters and the going was tougher all the time. Convinced that he could not break through, he called Colonel Moore and asked permission to pull back. The colonel gave it.

Captain Herren's situation was little better than Captain Nadal's. Having tried to advance from the creek bed by fire and maneuver, Herren too found his men engaged almost immediately and as a result had gained even less ground than Company A. Understrength at the outset of the operation, Herren had incurred thirty casualties by 1700. Although he was anxious to reach his cutoff platoon, he too held up his troops when he monitored Captain Nadal's message.

Colonel Moore had little choice as to Captain Nadal's request. The battalion was fighting in three separate actions—one force was defending X-RAY, two companies were attacking, and one platoon was isolated. To continue under these circumstances would be to risk the battalion's defeat in detail if the enemy discovered and capitalized on Moore's predicament. The forces at X-RAY were liable to heavy attack from other directions, and to continue to push Companies A and B against so tenacious an enemy was to risk continuing heavy casualties. The key to the battalion's survival, as Moore saw it, was the physical security of X-RAY itself, especially in the light of what the first prisoner had told him about the presence of three enemy battalions. Moore decided to pull his forces back, intending to attack again later that night or early in the morning or to order the platoon to attempt to infiltrate back to friendly lines.

But the move was not easy to make. Because of the heavy fighting, Company A's 1st Platoon had trouble pulling back with its dead and wounded. Captain Nadal committed the 3d Platoon to help relieve the pressure and assist with the casualties. Since he had lost his artillery forward observer, he requested through Colonel Moore artillery smoke on the company to screen its withdrawal. When Moore relayed the request, the fire direction center replied that smoke rounds were not available. Recalling his Korean War experience, Moore approved the use of white phosphorus instead. It seemed to dissuade the enemy; fire diminished immediately thereafter.

The success of the volley encouraged Nadal to call for another, which had a similar effect. Miraculously, in both instances, no friendly troops were injured, and both companies were able to break away.

By 1705 the 2d Platoon and command group of Company B, 2d Battalion, 7th Cavalry, were landing in X-RAY. Amidst cheers from the men on the ground, Capt. Myron Diduryk climbed out of the lead helicopter, ran up to Colonel Moore, and saluted with a "Gerry Owen, sir!" Colonel Moore briefed Diduryk on the tactical situation and then assigned him the role of battalion reserve and instructed him to be prepared to counterattack in either Company A, B, or C sector, with emphasis on the last one. An hour or so later, concerned about Company C's having the lion's share of the perimeter, Colonel Moore attached Diduryk's 2d Platoon to it.

Captain Diduryk's 120-man force was coming to the battle as well prepared as the 1st Battalion, 7th Cavalry, troops already there. Each rifleman had 15 to 20 magazines, and every M60 machine gun crew carried at least 4 boxes of ball ammunition. The 40-mm. grenadiers had 30 to 40 rounds each, and every man in the company carried at least 1 fragmentation grenade. In addition to a platoon-size basic load ammunition supply, Diduryk had two 81-mm. mortars and forty-eight high-explosive rounds.

When 2d Lt. James L. Lane, leader of the 2d Platoon, Company B, reported to Company C with his platoon for instructions, Captain Edwards placed him on the right flank of his perimeter where he could link up with Company A. Edwards directed all the men to dig prone shelters. Other than for close-in local security, Edwards established no listening posts. The thick elephant grass would cut down on their usefulness, and the protective artillery concentrations that he planned within a hundred meters of his line would endanger them.

Rather than dig in, Company A took advantage of the cover of the dry creek bed. Captain Nadal placed all his platoons in it, except for the four left flank positions of his 3d Platoon, which he arranged up on the bank where they could tie in with Company C.

Company B elected not to use the creek bed. Instead, Captain Herren placed his two depleted platoons just forward of it, along 150 meters of good defensive terrain, an average of five meters between positions, with his command post behind them in the creek bed. He began immediately to register his artillery concentrations as close as possible to his defensive line and ordered his men to dig in.

Company D continued to occupy its sector of the perimeter without change.

By 1800 all of Company B, 2d Battalion, 7th Cavalry, had landed. A half hour later Colonel Moore, figuring that the reconnaissance platoon was a large enough reserve force, readily available and positioned near the anthill, changed Captain Diduryk's mission, directing him to man the perimeter between Companies B and D with his remaining two platoons. 2d Lt. Cyril R. Rescorla linked his 1st Platoon with Company B, while 2d Lt. Albert E. Vernon joined his flank with Company D on his left. Diduryk placed his two 81-mm. mortars with the 1st Battalion, 7th Cavalry, and allowed some of the crew to man the perimeter. Soon his men were digging in, clearing fields of fire, and adjusting close-in concentrations.

Except for completing registration of artillery and mortar fire, Colonel Moore had organized his battalion perimeter by 1900. Fighting had long since died down to the tolerable level of sporadic sniper fire, and as night came on the last of the dead and wounded were being airlifted to FALCON from the collecting point in the vicinity of the battalion command post, near the anthill. Just before dark a resupply of much needed ammunition, water, medical supplies, and rations was flown in. The aid station had been dangerously low on dexadrine, morphine, and bandages and the water supply had reached such a critical stage at one point that a few soldiers had eaten C ration jam for its moisture content to gain relief from the heat. A two-ship zone for night landing was established in the northern portion of X-RAY. Although under enemy observation and fire, it was much less vulnerable than other sectors of X-RAY where most of the fighting had occurred.

At 1850 Colonel Moore radioed his S-3, Captain Dillon, to land as soon as possible with two more radio operators, the artillery liaison officer, the forward air controller, more small arms ammunition, and water. Except for refueling stops Dillon had been in the command helicopter above X-RAY continuously, monitoring the tactical situation by radio, relaying information to brigade headquarters, and passing on instructions to the rifle companies; the helicopter itself served as an aerial platform from which Captain Whiteside and Lieutenant Hastings directed the artillery fire and air strikes. In order to carry out Colonel Moore's instructions, Dillon requested two helicopters from FALCON. By 2125 Dillon was nearing X-RAY from the south through a haze of dust and smoke. Just as his helicopter approached for touchdown, he glanced to the left and saw what appeared to be four or five blinking lights on the forward slopes of Chu Pong. The lights hovered and wavered in the darkness. He surmised that they were North Vietnamese troops using flashlights to signal each other while they moved, for he recalled how an officer from another American division had reported a similar incident two months earlier during an operation in Binh Dinh Province. Upon landing, Dillon passed this information on to Whiteside and Hastings as target data.

During the early hours of darkness, Colonel Moore, accompanied by his sergeant major, made spot visits around the battalion perimeter, talking to the men. Although his troops were facing a formidable enemy force and had suffered quite a few casualties, their morale was clearly high. Moore satisfied himself that his companies were tied in, mortars were all registered, an ammunition resupply system had been established, and in general his troops were prepared for the night. (Map 3 overleaf)

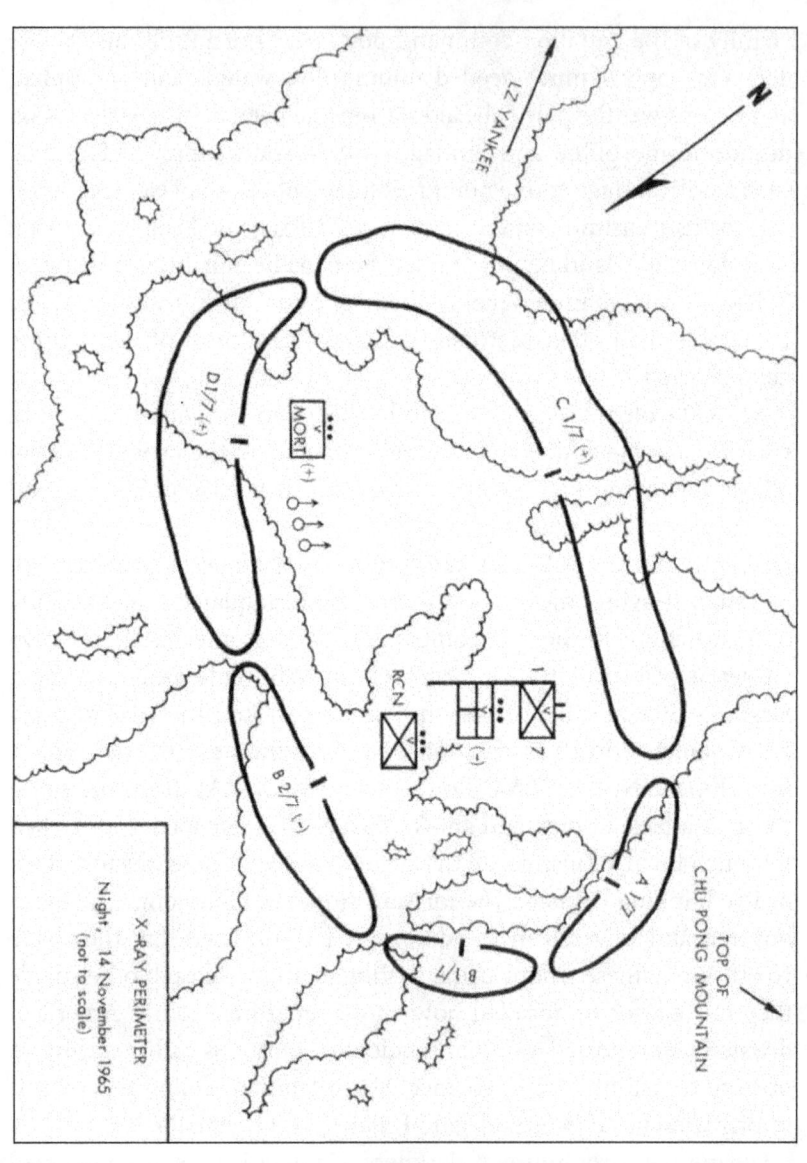

Map 3. X-RAY perimeter. Night, 14 November 1965

During the evening the 66th North Vietnamese Regiment moved its 8th Battalion southward from a position north of the Ia Drang and charged it with the mission of applying pressure against the eastern sector of X-RAY. Field Front headquarters meanwhile arranged for movement of the H-15 Main Force Viet Cong Battalion from an assembly area well south of the scene of the fighting. The 32d Regiment had not yet left its assembly area, some twelve kilometers away, and the heavy mortar and antiaircraft units were still en route to X-RAY.

At intervals during the night, enemy forces harassed and probed the battalion perimeter in all but the Company D sector, and in each instance well-placed American artillery from FALCON blunted the enemy's aggressiveness. Firing some 4,000 rounds, the two howitzer batteries in that landing zone also laced the fingers and draws of Chu Pong where the lights had been seen. Tactical air missions were flown throughout the night.

The remnants of Sergeant Savage's isolated little band meanwhile continued to be hard pressed. Three times the enemy attacked with at least a reinforced platoon but were turned back by the artillery and the small arms fire of the men in the perimeter, including some of the wounded. Spec. 5 Charles H. Lose, the company senior medical aidman (whom Captain Herren had placed with the platoon because of a shortage of medics), moved about the perimeter, exposed to fire while he administered to the wounded. His diligence and ingenuity throughout the day and during the night saved at least a half-dozen lives; having run out of first-aid packets as well as bandages from his own bag, he used the C ration toilet tissue packets most of the men had with them to help stop bleeding. Calm, sure, and thoroughly professional, he brought reassurance to the men.

Before the second attack, which came at 0345, bugle calls were heard around the entire perimeter. Some sounds seemed to come from Chu Pong itself, 200 to 400 meters distant. Sergeant Savage could even hear enemy soldiers muttering softly to each other in the sing-song cadence of their language. He called down a 15-minute artillery barrage to saturate the area and followed it with a tactical air strike on the ground just above the positions. Executed under flagship illumination, the two strikes in combination broke up the attack. The sergeant noted that the illumination exposed his position and it was therefore not used again that night.

A third and final attack came over an hour later and was as unsuccessful as the previous two. Sergeant Savage and his men, isolated but still holding throughout the night, could hear and sometimes see the enemy dragging off his dead and wounded.

At brigade headquarters, Colonel Brown continued to assess the significance of the day's activities. Pleased that the 1st Battalion, 7th Cavalry, had been able to hold its own against heavy odds, and with moderate casualties, he was convinced that the fight was not yet over. He radioed General Kinnard for another battalion, and Kinnard informed him that the 1st Battalion, 5th Cavalry, would begin arriving at brigade headquarters the following morning.

Having decided much earlier to try again for the third time to reach the isolated platoon and at the same time to secure the perimeter, Colonel Moore was ready by the next morning. Both he and his S-3 felt that the main enemy effort would be against the platoon. This time he intended to use three rifle companies instead of two. Since Captain Herren's men were most familiar with the ground, he planned to reinforce Company B with a platoon from Company A and to use Company B as the lead force again. Colonel Moore and his command group were to follow Herren's force. Companies A and C were to follow behind on the right and left, respectively, protecting the flanks and prepared to assist the main effort on order. The S-3, Captain Dillon, was to stay behind with the remainder of the battalion at the perimeter, ready to command it as a reserve force if necessary.

Ten minutes after first light, Colonel Moore directed all company commanders to meet him at the Company C command post where he would discuss final plans and view the attack route with them. He also told them to patrol forward and to the rear of their perimeter positions, looking for possible snipers or infiltrators that might have closed in during the night.

Upon receiving these instructions, Captain Edwards of Company C radioed his platoon leaders and told them to send at least squad size forces from each platoon out to a distance of 200 meters. No sooner had they moved out when heavy enemy fire erupted, shattering the morning stillness. The two leftmost reconnaissance elements, those of the 1st and 2d Platoons, took the brunt of the fire, which came mainly from their front and left front. They returned it and began pulling back to their defensive positions. Well camouflaged, and in some cases crawling on hands and knees, the North Vietnamese pressed forward. In short order the two reconnaissance parties began to suffer casualties, some of them fatal, while men in each of the other platoons were hit as they attempted to move forward to assist.

When he heard the firing, Captain Edwards immediately attempted to raise both the 1st and 2d Platoons on the radio for a situation report, but there was no answer; each platoon leader had accompanied the reconnaissance force forward. He called Lieutenant Lane, the attached platoon leader from Company B, 2d Battalion, and his 3d Platoon leader, 2d Lt. William W. Franklin, and was relieved to discover that most of their forces had made it back to the perimeter unscathed; a few were still attempting to help the men engaged with the enemy.

From his command post, Edwards himself could see fifteen to twenty enemy soldiers 200 meters to his front, moving toward him. He called Colonel Moore, briefed him on the situation, and requested artillery fire. Then he and the four others in his command group began firing their M16's at the advancing enemy. Edwards called battalion again and requested that the battalion reserve be committed in support.

Colonel Moore refused, for both he and Captain Dillon were still unconvinced that this was the enemy's main effort. They expected a strong attack against the isolated platoon and wanted to be prepared for it. Also, from what they could hear and see, Edwards' company appeared to be holding on, and they had given him priority of fires.

The situation of Company C grew worse, however, for despite a heavy pounding by artillery and tactical air and despite heavy losses the enemy managed to reach the foxhole line. Captain Edwards attempted to push Franklin's 3d Platoon to the left to relieve some of the pressure, but the firing was too heavy. Suddenly two North Vietnamese soldiers appeared forty meters to the front of the command post. Captain Edwards stood up and tossed a fragmentation grenade at them, then fell with a bullet in his back.

At 0715, seriously wounded but still conscious, Edwards asked again for reinforcements. This time Moore assented; he directed Company A to send a platoon. Company C's command group was now pinned down by an enemy automatic weapon that was operating behind an anthill just forward of the foxhole line. 2d Lt. John W. Arrington, Edwards' executive officer, had rushed forward from the battalion command post at Colonel Moore's order when Edwards was wounded.

As Arrington lay prone, receiving instructions from Captain Edwards, he was shot in the chest. Lieutenant Franklin, realizing that both his commanding officer and the executive officer had been hit, left his 3d Platoon position and began to crawl toward the command group. He was hit and wounded seriously.

Almost at the same time that the message from Edwards asking for assistance reached the battalion command post, the enemy also attacked the Company D sector in force near the mortar emplacements. The battalion was now being attacked from two different directions.

As soon as Captain Nadal had received the word to commit a platoon, he had pulled his right flank platoon, the 2d, for the mission since he did not want to weaken that portion of the perimeter nearest Company C. He ordered his remaining platoon to extend to the right and cover the gap. The 2d Platoon started across the landing zone toward the Company C sector. As it neared the battalion command post, moving across open ground, it came under heavy fire that wounded two men and killed two. The platoon deployed on line, everyone prone, in a position just a few meters behind and to the left of the 3d Platoon of Company A's left flank and directly behind Company C's right flank. The force remained where it had been stopped. It was just as well, for in this position it served adequately as a backup reserve, a defense in depth against any enemy attempt to reach the battalion command post.

The heavy fighting continued. At 0745 enemy grazing fire was crisscrossing X-RAY, and at least twelve rounds of rocket or mortar fire exploded in the landing zone. One soldier was killed near the anthill, others were wounded. Anyone who moved toward the Company C sector drew fire immediately. Still the men fought on ferociously. One rifleman from Company D, who during the fighting had wound up somehow in the Company C sector, covered fifty meters of ground and from a kneeling position shot ten to fifteen North Vietnamese with his M16.

Colonel Moore alerted the reconnaissance platoon to be prepared for possible commitment in the Company D or Company C sector. Next, he radioed Colonel Brown at brigade headquarters, informed him of the situation, and requested another reinforcing company. Colonel Brown approved the request and prepared to send Company A, 2d Battalion, 7th Cavalry, into the landing zone as soon as the intensity of the firing diminished.

At 0755 Moore directed all units to throw colored smoke grenades so that ground artillery, aerial rocket artillery, and tactical air observers could more readily see the perimeter periphery, for he wanted to get his fire support in as close as possible. As soon as the smoke was thrown, supporting fires were brought in extremely close. Several artillery rounds landed within the perimeter, and one F-105 jet, flying a northwest-southeast pass, splashed two tanks of napalm into the anthill area, burning some of the men, exploding M16 ammunition stacked in the area, and threatening to detonate a pile of hand grenades. While troops worked to put out the fire, Captain Dillon rushed to the middle of the landing zone under fire and laid out a cerise panel so that strike aircraft could better identify the command post.

Despite the close fire support, heavy enemy fire continued to lash the landing zone without letup as the North Vietnamese troops followed their standard tactic of attempting to mingle with the American defenders in order to neutralize American fire support. A medic was killed at the battalion command post as he worked on one of the men wounded during the napalm strike. One of Colonel Moore's radio operators was struck in the head by a bullet; he was unconscious for a half hour, but his helmet had saved his life.

By 0800 a small enemy force had jabbed at Company A's left flank and been repulsed, but Company D's sector was seriously threatened. Mortar crewmen were firing rifles as well as feeding rounds into their tubes when a sudden fusillade destroyed one of the mortars. The antitank platoon was heavily engaged at the edge of the perimeter. With the battalion under attack from three sides now, Colonel Moore shifted the reconnaissance platoon toward Company D to relieve some of the pressure there. He radioed Colonel Brown for the additional company and alerted Company B, 2d Battalion, 7th Cavalry, for action. He would have Company B on call until the battalion's Company A could put down in the landing zone.

Moore ordered Captain Diduryk to assemble his command group and his 1st Platoon at the anthill. Since he had already committed his 2d Platoon to Company C the previous night, Diduryk had left only the 3d Platoon to occupy his entire sector of the perimeter. He told the platoon leader, Lieutenant Vernon, to remain in position until relieved. Diduryk's 1st Platoon had lost one man wounded and one killed from the extremely heavy grazing fire and had not yet even been committed.

By 0900 the volume of combined American fires began to take its toll; enemy fire slacked. Ten minutes later, elements of Company A, 2d Battalion, 7th Cavalry, landed. Colonel Moore directed the company commander, Capt. Joel E. Sugdinis, to occupy Diduryk's original sector, which he did after co-ordinating with Diduryk.

By 1000 the enemy's desperate attempts to overwhelm the perimeter had failed and attacks ceased. Only light sniper fire continued. A half hour later Diduryk's company joined Lieutenant Lane's platoon in the Company C sector. Diduryk's force was augmented by the 3d Platoon of Company A, 2d Battalion, 7th Cavalry, which had rushed there immediately upon landing. Colonel Moore elected to allow it to remain.

Meanwhile, less than three kilometers southeast of the fighting, additional reinforcements were en route to X-RAY. Having departed Landing Zone VICTOR earlier that morning, Colonel Tully's 2d Battalion, 5th Cavalry, was moving on foot toward the sound of the firing.

Because of the scarcity of aircraft on 13 November as well as the dispersion of his companies over a relatively large area, Colonel Tally had been able to send only two of his companies into VICTOR before dark on the 14th. At that, it had been a major effort to get one of them, Company C, picked up and flown to VICTOR, so dense was the jungle cover. In clearing a two-helicopter pickup zone, the soldiers of Company C had used over thirty pounds of plastic explosive and had broken seventeen intrenching tools.

By the early morning hours of the 15th, Colonel Tully nevertheless had managed to assemble his three rifle companies in accordance with Colonel Brown's instructions. The task force moved out at 0800, Companies A and B abreast, left and right, respectively, with Company C trailing Company A. Colonel Tully used this formation, heavy on the left, because of the Chu Pong threat. He felt that if the enemy struck again it would be from that direction. He had no definite plan as to what he would do when he arrived at X-RAY other than reinforce. Details would come later.

Shortly after the fighting died down at X-RAY, enemy automatic weapons fire pinned down the two lead platoons of Company A, 2d

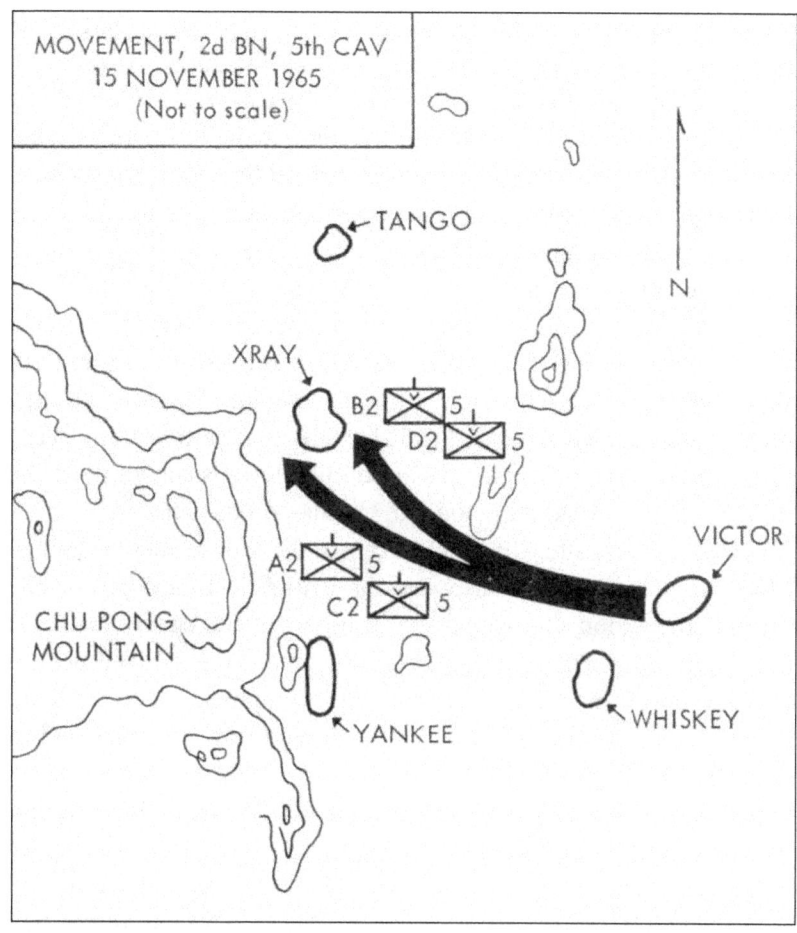

Map 4. Movement, 2d Battalion, 5th Cavalry, 15 November 1965

Battalion, 5th Cavalry, as they approached from the east, 800 meters from the landing zone. The North Vietnamese were in trees and behind anthills. The company commander, Capt. Larry T. Bennett, promptly maneuvered the two lead platoons, which were in a line formation, forward. Then he swung his 3d Platoon to the right flank and pushed ahead; his weapons platoon, which had been reorganized into a provisional rifle platoon, followed behind as reserve. The men broke through the resistance rapidly, capturing two young and scared North Vietnamese armed with AK47 assault rifles.

Soon after midday lead elements reached X-RAY. Colonel Moore and Colonel Tully co-ordinated the next move, agreeing that because they were in the best position for attack and were relatively fresh and strong upon arriving at the landing zone, Companies A and C, 2d Battalion, 5th Cavalry, would participate in the effort to reach the cutoff platoon. Company B, 1st Battalion, 7th Cavalry, would take the lead since Herren knew the terrain between X-RAY and the isolated platoon. Moore would receive Company B, 2d Battalion, 5th Cavalry, into the perimeter and would remain behind, still in command, while Colonel Tully accompanied the attack force. The incoming battalion's mortar sections were to remain at X-RAY and support the attack.

Colonel Tully's co-ordination with Captain Herren was simple enough. Tully gave Herren the appropriate radio frequencies and call signs, told him where to tie in with his Company A, and instructed him to move out when ready. At 1315, preceded by artillery and aerial rocket strikes, the rescue force started out, Herren's company on the right, Company A, 2d Battalion, 5th Cavalry, on the left.

Fifteen minutes after the relief force had left the perimeter, Colonel Moore directed all units to police the battlefield to a depth of 300 meters. They soon discovered the heavy price the enemy had paid for his efforts: enemy bodies littered the area, some stacked behind anthills; body fragments, weapons, and equipment were scattered about the edge of the perimeter; trails littered with bandages told of many bodies dragged away.

The cost had also been heavy for the 1st Battalion, 7th Cavalry, which had lost the equivalent of an American rifle platoon. The bodies of these men lay amongst the enemy dead and attested to the intensity of the fight. One rifleman of Company C lay with his hands clutched around the throat of a dead North Vietnamese soldier. Company C's 1st Platoon leader died in a foxhole surrounded by five enemy dead.

The relief party, meanwhile, advanced cautiously, harassed by sporadic sniper fire to which the infantrymen replied by judiciously calling down artillery fire. As they neared Sergeant Savage's platoon, lead troops of Captain Herren's company found the captured M60 machine gun, smashed by artillery fire. Around it lay the mutilated bodies of the crew, along with the bodies of successive North Vietnamese crews. They found the body of the M79 gunner, his .45-caliber automatic still clutched in his hand.

A few minutes later, the first men reached the isolated platoon; Captain Herren stared at the scene before him with fatigue-rimmed eyes. Some of the survivors broke into tears of relief. Through good fortune, the enemy's ignorance of their predicament, Specialist Lose's first-aid knowledge, individual bravery, and, most important of all, Sergeant Savage's expert use of artillery fire, the platoon had incurred not a single additional casualty after Savage had taken command the previous afternoon. Each man still had adequate ammunition.

Colonel Tully did not make a thorough search of the area, for now that he had reached the platoon his concern was to evacuate the survivors and casualties to X-RAY in good order. Accordingly, he surrounded the position with all three companies while Captain Herren provided details of men to assist with the casualties. The task was arduous, for each dead body and many of the wounded required at least a four-man carrying party using a makeshift poncho litter.

As he walked the newly established outer perimeter edge to check on the disposition of one of his platoons, Captain Bennett, the commander of Company A, 2d Battalion, 5th Cavalry, fell, severely wounded by a bullet in his chest fired at close range by a hidden North Vietnamese sniper. A thorough search for the enemy rifleman proved fruitless, and Colonel Tully directed his force to return to X-RAY. With Herren's company in single file and the casualties and Tully's units on either flank, the rescue force arrived at the landing zone without further incident.

Colonel Moore now redisposed his troops. Since he had two battalions to employ, he worked out an arrangement with Colonel Tully that allowed him to control all troops in the perimeter. He took Company D, minus the mortar platoon, off of the line and replaced it with Colonel Tully's entire battalion. Tully's force also occupied portions of the flanking unit sectors. The wounded and dead were evacuated and everyone dug in for the night.

That evening at brigade headquarters, Colonel Brown again conferred with General Kinnard, who told Brown that the 1st Battalion, 7th Cavalry, would be pulled out on the 16th and sent to Camp Holloway just outside Pleiku for two days of rest and reorganization.

Although the North Vietnamese had suffered heavy casualties, not only from their encounter with the 1st Battalion, 7th Cavalry, but also as a result of a B-52 strike on Chu Pong itself that afternoon, they had not abandoned the field entirely. Sporadic sniper fire continued at various points along the perimeter during the early part of the night. The moon was out by 2320 in a cloudless sky. American artillery fired continuously into areas around the entire perimeter and on Chu Pong where secondary explosions occurred during the early evening. At 0100 five North Vietnamese soldiers probed the Company B, 1st Battalion, 7th Cavalry, sector; two were killed and the others escaped. Three hours later, a series of long and short whistle signals were heard from the enemy, and a flurry of activity occurred in front of Company B, 2d Battalion, 7th Cavalry. Trip flares were ignited and anti-intrusion alarms sprung, some as far out as 300 meters. At 0422 Diduryk's attached Company A platoon leader, 2d Lt. William H. Sisson, radioed that he could see a group of soldiers advancing toward his positions. He was granted permission to fire and at the same time his platoon was fired on by the enemy. In less than ten minutes Diduryk was under attack along his entire sector by at least a company-size force. His company met the attack with a fusillade of fire from individual weapons, coupled with the firepower of four artillery batteries and all available mortars. Calling for point-detonating and variable time fazes, white phosphorus, and high-explosive shells, Diduryk's forward observer, 1st Lt. William L. Lund, directed each battery to fire different defensive concentrations in front of the perimeter, shifting the fires laterally and in depth in 100-meter adjustments. This imaginative effort, along with illumination provided by Air Force flareships, proved highly effective. Enemy soldiers nevertheless attempted to advance during the brief periods of darkness between flares and in some cases managed to get within five to ten meters of the foxhole line, where they were halted by well-aimed hand grenades and selective firing.

At 0530 the enemy tried again, this time shifting to the southwest, attacking the 3d Platoon and some left flank positions of the 2d Platoon. This effort, as well as another launched an hour later against the 1st Platoon's right flank, was also repulsed.

During the firelight, the Company B executive officer, radio operators, and troops from the reconnaissance platoon of the 1st Battalion, 7th Cavalry, made three separate ammunition resupply runs under fire to the anthill. At one point the supply of M79 ammunition dropped to such a dangerously low level that Diduryk restricted its use to visible targets, especially enemy crew-served weapons and troop concentrations.

By dawn of the 16th the enemy attack had run its course. Diduryk's company had only six men slightly wounded, while piles of enemy dead in front of the positions testified to the enemy's tactical failure.

Still concerned with possible enemy intentions and capabilities and no doubt wary because of what had happened to Company C on the previous morning's sweep, Colonel Moore directed all companies to spray the trees, anthills, and bushes in front of their positions to kill any snipers or other infiltrators—a practice that the men called a "mad minute." Seconds after the firing began, an enemy platoon-size force came into view 150 meters in front of Company A, 2d Battalion, 7th Cavalry, and opened fire at the perimeter. An ideal artillery target, the attacking force was beaten off in twenty minutes by a heavy dose of high-explosive variable time fire. The "mad minute" effort proved fruitful in other respects. During the firing one North Vietnamese soldier dropped from a tree, dead, immediately in front of Captain Herren's command post. The riddled body of another fell and hung upside down, swinging from the branch to which the man had tied himself in front of Diduryk's leftmost platoon. An hour later somebody picked off an enemy soldier as he attempted to climb down a tree and escape.

Company C, 1st Battalion, 7th Cavalry, and the reconnaissance platoon meanwhile made a detailed search of the interior of X-RAY itself. There were three American casualties unaccounted for, and Colonel Moore was still concerned about infiltrators. The search turned up nothing.

An hour later, Moore considered it opportune to push out from the perimeter on a co-ordinated search and to sweep out to 500 meters. The move commenced at 0955. After covering fifty to seventy-five meters, Company B, 2d Battalion, 7th Cavalry, platoons met a large volume of fire, including hand grenades thrown by enemy wounded still lying in the area. Diduryk quickly lost a weapons squad leader killed and nine other men wounded, including the 2d Platoon leader and platoon sergeant. Under artillery cover, he withdrew his force to the perimeter. Colonel Moore and Lieutenant Hastings, the forward air controller, joined him. A few minutes later tactical air, using a variety of ordnance that included rockets, cannon, napalm, cluster bomb units, white phosphorus, and high explosive, blasted the target area. The strike ended with the dropping of a 500-pound bomb that landed only twenty-five meters from the 1st Platoon's positions.

The sweep by Company B, 2d Battalion, 7th Cavalry, began again, this time using fire and maneuver behind a wall of covering artillery fire and meeting scattered resistance which was readily eliminated. Twenty-seven North Vietnamese were killed. The sweep uncovered the three missing Americans, all dead. The area was littered with enemy dead, and many enemy weapons were collected.

By 0930 the lead forces of the remainder of the 2d Battalion, 7th Cavalry, reached X-RAY, and an hour later Colonel Moore received instructions to prepare his battalion, along with Company B, 2d Battalion, 7th Cavalry, and the 3d Platoon, Company A, 2d Battalion, 7th Cavalry, for the move to Camp Holloway. The remainder of the 2d Battalion, 7th Cavalry, and 2d Battalion, 5th Cavalry, were to be left behind to secure the perimeter. Moore did not want to leave, however, without another thorough policing of the battle area, particularly where Company C had been attacked on the morning of the 15th. Captain Diduryk therefore conducted a lateral sweep without incident to a distance of 150 meters.

As the 1st Battalion, 7th Cavalry, began its move to Camp Holloway, the casualties with their equipment, as well as the surplus supplies, were also evacuated. Captured enemy equipment taken out included 57 Kalashnikov AK47 assault rifles, 54 Siminov SKS semiautomatic carbines with bayonets, 17 Degtyarev automatic rifles, 4 Maxim heavy machine guns; 5 model RPG2 antitank rocket launchers; 2 81-mm. mortar tubes, 2 pistols, and 6 medic's kits.

Great amounts of enemy weapons and equipment had been previously destroyed elsewhere in the battle area, and Moore arranged with the commanding officer of the 2d Battalion, 7th Cavalry, to destroy any enemy materiel left behind at X-RAY. Included were 75 to 100 crew-served and individual weapons, 12 antitank rounds, 300 to 400 hand grenades, an estimated 5,000 to 7,000 small arms rounds, and 100 to 150 entrenching tools.

American casualties, attached units included, were 79 killed, 121 wounded, and none missing. Enemy losses were much higher and included 634 known dead, 581 estimated dead, and 6 prisoners.

2. Convoy Ambush on Highway 1 21 November 1966

BY JOHN ALBRIGHT

When the 11th Armored Cavalry—the "Blackhorse Regiment"—arrived in the Republic of Vietnam in September 1966, the threat of ambush hung over every highway in the country. Since the regiment's three squadrons each had a company of main battle tanks, three armored cavalry troops, and a howitzer battery, the Blackhorse was well suited for meeting the challenge.

Each of the cavalry troop's three platoons had nine armored cavalry assault vehicles (ACAV's). The ACAV was an M113 armored personnel carrier modified for service in Vietnam and particularly adapted to convoy escort. With the M113's usual complement of one .50-caliber machine gun augmented by two M60 machine guns, all protected by armored gun shields, and with one of its five-man crew armed with a 40-mm. grenade launcher, the vehicle took on some of the characteristics of a light tank. Fast, the track-laying ACAV could keep pace with wheeled vehicles and also deliver withering fire.

Aware that convoy escort would be a primary mission of the 11th Cavalry, the regiment's leaders had concentrated in the five months between alert and departure for Vietnam on practicing counter ambush techniques. In countless mock ambushes, the cavalrymen learned to react swiftly with fire. The first object was to run thin-skinned vehicles out of the killing zone; the armored escorts would then return to roll up the enemy's flanks, blasting with every weapon and crushing the enemy beneath their tracks.

In mid-October, a month after arriving at a staging area at Long Binh, a few kilometers northeast of Saigon, the regiment issued its first major operational order. The Blackhorse was to establish a regimental base camp on more than a square mile of ground along Interprovincial Highway 2, twelve kilometers south of the provincial capital of Xuan Loc. (See Map 1 on page 8)

Even as the tanks and ACAV's entered and cleared the site for the

49

Armored cavalry assault vehicle

base, leaflets were dropped from helicopters onto nearby hamlets to alert villagers that the Blackhorse soldiers had come to stay. As the days passed, convoy after convoy rumbled through Xuan Loc on National Highway 1, then south on Highway 2 and on to the developing base camp. Always escorted by ACAV's, the convoys kept this stretch of National 1 open to a degree unknown since the beginning of the Viet Cong insurgency.

While work on the base camp continued, two of the 11th Cavalry's three squadrons were called far afield to assist in other operations. Since the remaining squadron was engaged in searching and clearing surrounding jungles, only company-size units remained to provide perimeter security for the camp. By mid-November the developing base, fat with military supplies of all kinds, had become an inviting target, lightly defended and still only lightly fortified.

Intelligence reports in early November indicated that the 5th Viet Cong Division, which had been fighting to dominate the Xuan Loc area and close Highway 1, was assuming the offensive. When word came that enemy troops had left their usual hideout south of Xuan Loc and were headed in the direction of the base camp, the 11th

Cavalry's commander, Col. William W. Cobb, asked for the return of one of his detached squadrons. The request granted, the 1st Squadron began arriving at Long Binh in late afternoon of 20 November on the first leg of a move to the base camp.

Although the howitzer battery and Troop A moved on immediately to augment defenders of the base camp, the rest of the squadron paused overnight at Long Binh to "top off" with fuel and "pull maintenance." These men would leave early the next morning, after a convoy taking along staff sections, clerks, cooks, medics, and other support troops from regimental headquarters had arrived at the camp.

As night fell on 20 November, the two forces that would fight the next day drew closer together. The last vehicles of the 1st Squadron closed at Long Binh in a heavy rain, their crews tired from a 12-hour road march at the end of almost two weeks in the field. Rain continued to pour while the support troops loaded supplies and equipment into the trucks that were to join the convoy the next morning. At the same time, the monsoon that drenched the troopers of the Blackhorse pelted the two battalions and headquarters of the 5th Viet Cong Division's 274th Regiment—the battle-hardened Dong Nai Regiment—as they moved into ambush positions along National Highway 1, west of Xuan Loc.

Midway between the provincial capitals of Bien Hoa and Xuan Loc, Highway 1 dropped sharply to a stream bed and then rose to a gently rolling plateau. A dirt road running north and south intersected National Highway 1 at this point. Low hills rising only 10 to 20 meters above the road level began about 180 meters from the highway on both sides.

On the north side of the highway, grass high enough to hide a standing man covered the ground. Rising like an island in the sea of grass was an expanse of jungle 1,000 meters square, beginning at the north-south dirt road and running parallel to Highway 1,300 meters north of the edge of the highway.

Along the south side of the highway a wall of jungle had grown up around the trees of an old rubber plantation stretching from the province boundary east for 1,000 meters and ending abruptly at a banana grove. The banana grove lined the south side of the highway for 300 meters before it gave way to an open area ending at the hamlet of Ap Hung Nghia.

Because the jungle and banana grove offered concealment for

approach and withdrawal, the commander of the Viet Cong 274th Regiment placed his main force of over a thousand men on the south side of the road, camouflaged and ready to fire automatic weapons and antitank rockets point-blank onto the highway. The ambush extended from just inside the west end of the jungle to the outskirts of Ap Hung Nghia, a distance of 1,500 meters. To handle any U.S. troops who might dismount and take refuge on the north side of the road, the Viet Cong commander deployed infantrymen alone or in groups of two or three across the highway in the tall grass.

In the classic manner of Viet Cong ambush forces, heavy weapons marked both ends of the killing zone. A 75-mm. recoilless rifle, positioned less than fifteen feet from the road, marked the beginning of the killing zone, just twenty feet inside the west end of the jungle close by the banana grove. A second 75-mm. recoilless rifle dominated the road in the eastern half of the killing zone from the forward slope of a slight hill just to the east of the banana grove. A 57-mm. recoilless rifle farther up the hill, three hundred meters to the east, and an 82-mm. mortar deep in the jungle were to provide supporting fire. Heavy machine guns hidden in huts scattered through the killing zone were to engage American helicopters and jets. Regimental headquarters operated on the crest of a hill five hundred meters west of Ap Hung Nghia, overlooking the entire section of road in the killing zone.

Once the ambush was executed the 274th Regiment was to withdraw to railroad tracks parallel to and a thousand meters south of the highway, then along a trail leading due south under a heavy canopy of jungle. Bunkers along the trail for a distance of two kilometers would provide cover against air attack, while bunkers at the beginning of the trail and a hundred meters south of the railroad tracks would provide defensive positions for a delaying force.

Through the wet chilly night of 20 November, men of the Dong Nai Regiment waited in their concealed positions.

At Long Binh loading of the convoy continued well into the night. Tents housing staff sections were struck, folded, and loaded dripping wet into the waiting trucks. Some drivers then put their trucks in line along the road near the convoy's starting point in the hope of being near the front of the column where they could avoid at least some of the grime and exhaust fumes that would plague others farther to the rear.

Hoisting CONEX container for convoy loading

By 0600, most of the trucks waited at the starting point, though stragglers and latecomers in a variety of vehicles continued to join the column until almost 0700, the announced starting time. Yet 0700 passed and still the escorts had not arrived; one of those inexplicable waits that always seem to haunt units on the move now set in. After a while support units and staff sections that had assumed they could not be ready to leave with the morning convoy saw their chance. They quickly finished loading and lined up their vehicles at the rear of the column. A long column grew longer. Five-ton trucks carrying document-filled CONEX containers (steel cargo transporters), S and P's (stake and platform trucks) loaded with small prefabricated buildings and supplies, jeeps and their trailers, 34-ton trucks, 2¼-ton "deuce and a half's," and even two large ordnance vans loaded with post exchange supplies and the regiment's finance records, a most precious cargo, joined the column.

Word filtered down through the convoy that the column would roll at eight, then at nine. But not until 0840 was the convoy escort commander designated 1st Lt. Neil L. Keltner, commanding the 1st Platoon, Troop C, of the 1st Squadron.

Keltner quickly gathered the vehicles for his escort, four ACAV's from his platoon and four from Troop C's 2d Platoon. He found, sandwiched among the trucks, an ACAV from Troop A that had missed that troop's move the preceding day. This ACAV—numbered A34—he quickly integrated into his escort force.

He might need this additional armor and more, Keltner mused, for with the help of Capt. Robert Smith, the forward air controller who was circling above the ever-lengthening line, Keltner estimated that the convoy now consisted of over eighty vehicles "of about every size and shape in the U.S. Army inventory."

For the march, Keltner placed his ACAV's in pairs: a pair at the head and rear of the column and at two points equidistant within the column. He added his own vehicle to the two—one of them was the A34 from Troop A—that were some twenty trucks behind the head of the convoy.

At 0920 Lieutenant Keltner gave the signal: "Move out."

Rising from the grass along the road where they had been dozing, truckers and their passenger's donned flak jackets, put on helmets, picked up their weapons, and mounted their vehicles. Engines came to life all along the line and the convoy began to roll. After traveling less than a mile, the lead vehicle turned onto National Highway 1 and passed through the village of Ho Nai. The men aboard could not know it but at this point a Viet Cong observation post somewhere in Ho Nai flashed word to the 274th Regiment that the convoy was on the way.

Haphazardly formed, lacking unit integrity, the convoy was by its very nature difficult to protect. Great gaps within the column began to develop early as lightly laden vehicles pulled far ahead of heavily loaded trucks. Accordion-like, the line stretched.

The convoy had been on the road less than forty-five minutes when a non-commissioned officer, M. Sgt. Joseph Smolenski, at the 11th Cavalry's tactical operational center, received an intelligence message in the form of a code word and a location. Instantly recognizing the code word as one the intelligence staff had been told to watch for, he rushed the communication to Maj. Grail L. Brookshire, the regimental S-2. Brookshire realized at once that the message indicated the presence of the headquarters of the 274th Regiment, the best combat unit in the 5th Viet Cong Division. As revealed by the co-ordinates, the enemy location was fifteen kilometers west of Xuan Loc, along Highway I and near Ap Hung Nghia. Confirming that a convoy was on the road, the S-2 saw the position of the enemy troops for what it was—an ambush.

Only a minute passed after receipt of the message before the S-2 radioed a warning of the enemy location to the 1st Squadron's operations center at Long Binh. At the same time the assistant S-3, Capt. Harlen E. Gray, ordered the Blackhorse light fire team (two armed Huey helicopters) aloft to cover the convoy. With a "Witco" received from Blackhorse flight operations on the order, Captain Gray alerted the 1st Squadron on the regimental command net, re-enforcing the warning of a minute before on the intelligence net and using the 2d Squadron, located five kilometers nearer to the 1st Squadron's operations center, as a relay station.

While commanders and duty officers at the two headquarters frantically worked to protect the convoy, the object of their concern continued to rumble eastward toward Xuan Loc, with the forward air controller circling overhead. No warning had yet been sent to the convoy commander. Lieutenant Keltner's major concern remained the accordion-like motion of the convoy and the large gaps that constantly appeared in the column.

Dodging 55-gallon drums placed in the road to slow traffic, the lead trucks rolled through a Vietnamese National Police checkpoint midway between Bien Hoa and Xuan Loc, the men on the trucks waving to the policemen. Lieutenant Keltner's ACAV in the second group of escort vehicles was within a thousand meters of the ambush site when his radio crackled with a message from 1st Squadron headquarters.

"Suspected enemy activity at coordinates 289098."

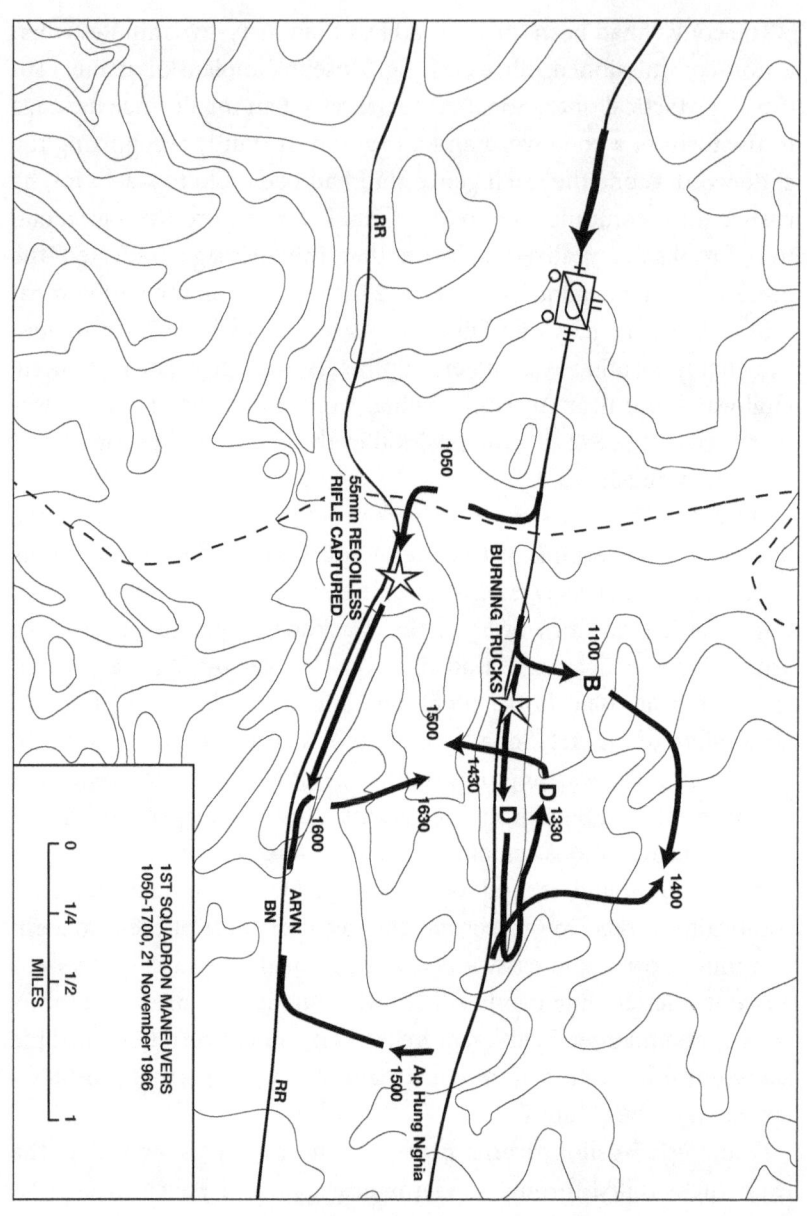

Map 5. 1st Squadron maneuvers, 1050–1700, 21 November 1966

It was a routine enough message, delivered in a matter-of-fact manner. The lieutenant asked for more information. Squadron headquarters had none. Keltner had received similar messages before and the enemy each time had failed to show up. He was not particularly worried about this one, but he immediately radioed the air controller to verify the location of the front of the column and the relation of the lead vehicles to the suspected enemy position.

Two controllers were by this time circling overhead; since Captain Smith's fuel was low, Maj. Mario J. Stefanelli had arrived to relieve him. Both officers already were alert to the possible enemy activity, for less than two minutes before Keltner received the message from his squadron Captain Smith had received a coded message from the 11th Cavalry operations center with the same information. As Smith finished copying the message, Major Stefanelli assumed air controller responsibility for the convoy, allowing Smith to decode the co-ordinates undisturbed. Smith still had enough fuel to stay overhead a few minutes longer. He was just finishing his decoding when Keltner's call reached Major Stefanelli.

The head of the convoy, Stefanelli answered, had just passed the suspected enemy location.

Keltner quickly radioed his ACAV's to warn them of the imminent danger. All but the lead ACAV—C22—answered. A few seconds later C22 reported receiving fire from small arms and automatic weapons and asked permission to return fire. Even as Keltner gave the permission, his own vehicle came alongside the edge of the banana grove that lay south of the highway, and Keltner informed squadron headquarters that the convoy was under fire. It was 1025.

Reacting to earlier counter ambush training, Lieutenant Keltner decided to run the column through the small arms fire. From the report of the lead ACAV he believed that the fire was but a harassing tactic, or at the most that it came from only a platoon or a company of Viet Cong. In any case, with eighty vehicles to protect and only nine ACAV's to do the job, Keltner felt he had little choice. (Map 5)

Still on the move, he ordered his own crew to spray the banana trees south of the road with fire. Just as his machine guns opened up, a mortar round burst close behind his ACAV and immediately in front of the next A34 but did no damage. While all the ACAV's of the first two groups poured machine gun fire into both sides of the road, nearly half of the convoy, including Keltner's own vehicle, passed safely through and beyond the killing zone. But the full force of the enemy's ambush still had not been brought to bear. Even though Keltner had received the warning too late to stop the column short of the killing zone, he had been able to alert his escorts almost at the exact moment the Viet Cong moved to spring their ambush. The Dong Nai Regiment had been denied the benefit of total surprise.

At Long Binh Lt. Col. Martin D. Howell, the squadron commander, heard Keltner report small arms fire. Like the lieutenant, he believed it to be harassing fire but nevertheless dispatched the remainder of Troop C to the scene. With Charley Troop roaring out of the staging area and the light fire team helicopters, alerted earlier, rushing to the scene, help was on the way even before the battle reached a peak.

Although most of the front half of the convoy had passed out of danger, eight trucks had fallen behind because the first of the eight was carrying a heavy load. As these last trucks and the section led by the next two ACAV's—C18 and C13—entered the killing zone, the ACAV's fired first into the edge of the jungle and, as they kept moving, into the banana grove. The Viet Cong answered with small arms and automatic weapons from both sides of the road. The exchange of fire at a range of less than twenty meters became a deafening roar. To many of the men in the following trucks, this fusillade was the first warning of an ambush, for vehicle noises had drowned out the earlier exchange. The trucks not yet under fire began to slow down, their drivers displaying the uncertainty they felt about what lay ahead.

Yet the convoy kept moving and the road ahead remained clear. The exchange of fire grew in volume as those trucks with "shotgun" riders began to engage the ambushers on the right (south) side of the road. The crash of exploding grenades added to the noise of battle. Then a round from a recoilless rifle struck C18 on the edge of the loading ramp but failed to stop the ACAV.

As the firelight continued at close range, the trucks forming the rear of the column, not yet in the killing zone, began to pull over to the side of the road. Those immediately behind C18 and C13, already under fire, stopped and the men aboard raced for cover in ditches on either side of the road. The only vehicles moving at that point were the last eight trucks from the first half of the column and ACAV's C13 and C18.

Hardly had C18 escaped one round from a recoilless rifle when another burned a hole in its right side, starting a fire. This hit wounded the ACAV commander, but the crew continued to fire the .50-caliber machine gun and the M60's into the enemy position south of the road.

Now another recoilless rifle round struck the heavily loaded lead truck whose slowness had opened a gap in the truck column. The gasoline tank exploded, instantly killing the two men in the cab. The truck lurched to the left into the ditch on the north side of the road, its trailer still on the pavement, partially blocking the highway. A column of thick black smoke shot into the morning sky. While the crew of C18 continued to fire, the wounded commander radioed his situation to Keltner. After passing the word on to squadron headquarters, Lieutenant Keltner turned around to enter the fight again, but before he could return C18 burst into flames. On order of the critically wounded sergeant, all the crew except the driver evacuated the vehicle, dragging the sergeant out of the commander's hatch and carrying him into the high grass on the north side of the highway. Only light fire had come from that direction, and it seemed the safest place to go. The driver of the burning C18 finally got it started again and headed down the road through a hail of small arms and antitank rocket fire, hoping to distract the enemy's attention and allow the other crewmen to make good their escape. He succeeded, but four hundred meters down the road met his death when one of the thousands of small arms rounds fired at the moving ACAV found its mark.

Even as C18 fought to the death, the troopers in C13, a few meters farther forward along the road, moved to counter small arms fire and grenades raining on the three remaining trucks to their front. Racing forward, the driver interposed his ACAV between the trucks and heavy enemy fire coming from the banana grove on the right side of the road, but not before a recoilless rifle sent a second truck up in flames.

As C13 came abreast of the burning truck, another round exploded against its right gun shield, destroying the M60 machine gun, killing the gunner, and wounding everybody but the driver. A recoilless rifle round struck the engine compartment and C13 began to burn. Although the driver himself was now wounded, he continued to move forward, deeper into the killing zone. Veering past the truck trailer that partially blocked the road; he went fifteen hundred meters past the end of the ambush. Only then did the crew abandon the burning vehicle. Moments later C13 exploded.

After C13 had rolled down the highway spewing smoke, there was a sudden silence. For the first time the men who had taken cover in the ditches alongside the road could hear jet fighters circling overhead and hear as well as see a flight of helicopters turning to make firing runs. The silence on the ground lasted perhaps ten seconds before it was broken by the roar of another round from a recoilless rifle aimed at one of the trucks that the trailer of the lead truck had blocked. So close was the range that the crash of the impacting round mingled with the roar of the backblast. Then came another blast, and a third, and a fourth, as the Viet Cong gunners methodically destroyed two more trucks.

The men replied with fierce counter fire. Sharply conscious that no ACAV's remained in the killing zone to provide fire support, they fully expected the Viet Cong to emerge from their ambush and overrun the ditch. But the enemy was feeling the air attacks. The column of smoke from the burning trucks was a beacon upon which air support was converging.

A minute after the first truck was hit, the two forward air controllers attacked with the only weapons they had—white phosphorus marking rockets. Flying their slow observation craft through heavy small arms fire, they searched for the Viet Cong. Seeing puffs of smoke from weapons firing in the banana grove; Major Stefanelli placed his first rocket there. His ship hit by ground fire but still operational, Captain Smith aimed his rocket into the jungle opposite the burning trucks. As Stefanelli fired a second rocket into the banana trees, Smith aimed his at a group of twenty Viet Cong who had risen and were running south. Even as the first trucks were hit and the first rockets struck, the ambush was breaking up.

When the two light aircraft pulled out of their diving attacks, the only Huey gunship operational with the 1st Squadron that day moved in. From having monitored the 1st Platoon's radio frequency, the pilot, Capt. Turner L. Nelson, knew almost as much about what was happening on the ground as did Lieutenant Keltner. He made two passes, firing machine guns and a total of eight rockets into the ambush positions. So heavy did the ground fire directed at the lone helicopter seem to the truckers in the ditches that few believed the ship could escape; somehow the helicopter emerged unscathed.

Close behind Captain Nelson's strikes came the regimental light fire team, alerted only minutes before. Diverted from an administrative mission in mid-flight, the team commander, Capt. George E. Kinback, approached the scene from the south. The second helicopter, piloted by Capt. Frank Y. Sasaki, had taken off from the Blackhorse helipad at the base camp and approached from the east. About three kilometers south of Highway 1, Kinback observed Sasaki's ship and directed him toward the column of smoke rising from the first of the stricken trucks.

As the two ships lined up for their first firing run, Kinback tried unsuccessfully to get instructions from Keltner by radio. Captain Nelson, circling north of the road, was unable to contact either Kinback or Sasaki. Yet lack of communications imposed little delay, for not only could Kinback and Sasaki spot the burning trucks, but heavy fire from the Viet Cong positions gave away the enemy's location.

On the first pass the two Hueys loosed machine gun fire and six pairs of rockets at the Viet Cong. On the second pass they had help from Captain Nelson, who was at last in communication with the team and fell in behind the regimental gunships. On this run the three Hueys poured continuous machine gun fire and nine pairs of rockets into the enemy positions. On a third and then a fourth firing run they expended the remaining six pairs of rockets and continued to hit the foe with machine gun fire.

While the fourth helicopter firing run was in progress, the regimental operations center radioed an order for the team to move north of the road to make way for a strike by Air Force jets. The arrival of jets in a battle only eight minutes old brought pure joy to those men of the convoy who were still crouching in the ditches. Three F-100's now joined the fight. The men on the ground had no way of knowing—nor would they have really cared—that they got this support less by calculated design than by a lucky break. An air controller on a routine administrative flight had seen the smoke of the first burning truck. Knowing that a preplanned air strike for a nearby South Vietnamese Army division was minutes away, he called the Blackhorse operations center and offered to turn the fighters over to the 11th Cavalry. The Blackhorse air liaison officer on duty at the center, Air Force Maj. Charles F. Post, had jumped at this unexpected windfall and informed Major Stefanelli. But even before the radio alerted them, the jets were roaring over the ambush, guided by the column of smoke. Reaching the fighter pilots on a universal emergency frequency, Stefanelli turned them over to Captain Smith, who had just enough fuel left to put the strike in before heading for home base.

The air liaison officer at the Blackhorse operations center directed the aircraft to strike fifty meters inside the jungle, south of the highway. Smith added a 25-meter safety margin, rolled his aircraft over, dived, and fired one of his two remaining marking rockets. Plunging through intense fire from the enemy, the jets dropped six high-drag 500-pound bombs at the western edge of the ambush. Smith then marked for a napalm run, and the jets dropped six tanks on more enemy troops running south; they followed with a strafing run of 20-mm. cannon fire on Viet Cong fleeing along a trail in the jungle south of the road.

As the air strike took place, Lieutenant Keltner, on the ground, was directing the commander of his lead ACAV to take that part of the convoy that had escaped the ambush on to the base camp. He himself turned his vehicle along with C10 back toward the burning trucks. Coming first upon C13, burning on the road, Keltner directed C10 to remain with the wounded crewmen who had taken cover in the high grass on the north side of the road until a helicopter could arrive. Then C10 would rejoin Keltner.

Alone, Keltner's ACAV pressed on at top speed toward the burning trucks, the lieutenant in the process radioing for a medical evacuation helicopter for the wounded. A helicopter from the Blackhorse base camp, already overhead and monitoring Keltner's frequency, responded immediately.

As Keltner's ACAV sped along the highway, ten Viet Cong suddenly darted across its path. Both the Viet Cong and the gunners in the ACAV opened fire. Five of the enemy fell; the others made it into the scrub jungle south of the road. Keltner's left machine gunner, hit in the head, died instantly. During this brief engagement a 57-mm. recoilless rifle fired five rounds at the lieutenant's vehicle. Despite the speed of C16—thirty-five to forty-five miles an hour—the last round hit its left side. Although the antitank round failed to stop Keltner's ACAV, the lieutenant and his right machine gunner were wounded by fragments and the intercom and radios were knocked out, leaving Keltner only a portable radio lashed to the outside of the commander's hatch. Intended for maintaining contact with the air controller, this radio provided the only remaining link between Keltner and his platoon.

When he reached the abandoned and still-smouldering hulk of C18, Keltner could detect no sign of the crew. He stopped long enough to remove the vehicle's machine guns, then drove on till he reached the burning trucks. From the ditch along the south side of the road, the men from the trucks were still exchanging small arms fire with the Viet Cong. Five to six minutes had passed since C13 and C18 had been knocked out. Calling for a second medical helicopter for the wounded truck drivers, Keltner rode down the line of trucks to make certain he had missed no casualties. Finding none, he continued to the rear of the convoy, where he left his dead gunner and exchanged his ACAV for C23 which had an operable intercom and radios.

Mounted in C23 and accompanied by C16, Keltner returned to the burning trucks, his gunners firing from the moving vehicle into the jungle. When the men from the trucks told him that most of the enemy fire was now coming from the north, Keltner radioed for an air strike against the edge of the jungle lying north of the highway. This call coincided with the end of the strafing run by the F-100's, but in response to a request by the 1st Squadron operations center, initiated only minutes after the ambush was sprung, two F-5 Freedom Fighters had arrived over the ambush site. They swept in on the target, hitting the west edge of the patch of jungle with cluster bomb units that sounded like rolling thunder to the troops along the edge of the road.

Observing the strike while cruising along the road with his machine gunners firing into the jungle on either side, Keltner called in an adjustment to Colonel Howell, who had arrived overhead in a Huey, and on the second pass the aircraft dropped napalm tanks closer to the south edge of the jungle. This did the job; no further enemy fire came from the north.

After another quick but unsuccessful search for the crew of C18, Keltner returned again to the burning trucks even as the first of the relief forces began to arrive.

When Colonel Howell had reacted to Lieutenant Keltner's first report of small arms fire by ordering Troop C to the scene, he had some qualms that he might be sending troops to deal with only a few snipers. But when Keltner's report of burning trucks came a few moments later, Howell ordered both Troop B and Company D (a tank company) to follow Troop C. As the squadron moved, Colonel Howell mounted his waiting helicopter. As soon as he gained altitude he could see the column of smoke from the trucks and the bombs of the air strike rising from the killing zone.

Guiding on the smoke, the colonel was soon over the ambush site, talking to Keltner, adjusting the second air strike, and formulating his battle plan. Troop C would go south of the highway and then east along the railroad tracks, cutting off the most obvious route of retreat, while Troop B would swing north in an arc connecting each end of the ambush. The tanks of Company D would push along the highway to force the enemy into the encircling troops.

As the relief force drew closer to the ambush, Colonel Howell and Lieutenant Keltner adjusted the second air strike to be brought against the enemy positions. Minutes later, Troop B swung north through the strike zone, Troop C turned south, and Company D's tanks swept into the grass north of the highway. It was 1100, only thirty-five minutes since the ambush had struck, and the squadron already had travelled over twenty kilometers.

While the squadron maneuvered, Keltner searched again for C18's missing crew. This time he found the men in the grass north of the road protecting their critically wounded commander. Within a few minutes a helicopter had evacuated them.

Twenty minutes after the relief force arrived, the southern pincer made contact with the enemy as 1st Lt. James V. Stewart fired at what proved to be the rear guard of the 274th Regiment, fleeing south across the railroad tracks. Stewart's crew killed two Viet Cong and captured a Chinese-made 57-mm. recoilless rifle. For the rest of the day the tanks and ACAV's continued closing the circle around the ambush site. Cruising through the grass adjacent to the highway, Company D flushed out and killed, one at a time, five Viet Cong. Troop A, released from the base camp, joined the squadron and killed one enemy soldier, and Troop B captured another. By 1600 it became clear that, even with the help of a South Vietnamese infantry battalion that made a cursory search of the area, the squadron had failed to trap the main force of the enemy.

Colonel Howell then directed the squadron to coil around the ambush site for the night.

After encountering a few enemy patrols that night, the squadron searched the battlefield the next day and for two days following. The men found bunkers along the escape route and a total of thirty enemy dead. The convoy and its escort had lost seven men killed and eight wounded, four trucks and two ACAV's destroyed.

From the beginning, the battle had not gone well for the Viet Cong. The ambush, designed to open with the crash of recoilless rifle fire and grenades, had begun with the sputter of small arms fire while half the convoy sped through unscathed. Alerted, most of the men had entered the killing zone firing into the jungle on both sides of the road. Not until the middle of the convoy reached the killing zone had the enemy fired heavy weapons. Almost from the first, Blackhorse helicopters had struck from the sky. The ACAV—new to the men of the Dong Nai Regiment, who had never seen a vehicle quite like it—poured more fire into the Viet Cong ranks than any other "personnel carrier" they had met. The clincher had come when the Ho Nai outpost flashed word that the relief force was on the way just minutes after the ambush struck; the regimental commander, whose troops were already beginning to flee south as jets came in to bomb, was obliged to order withdrawal when the fight had scarcely begun.

Late in the afternoon of 24 November—Thanksgiving Day—the squadron returned to the Blackhorse base camp.

National Highway 1 remained open.

3. Ambush at Phuoc An
18 June 1967

BY JOHN A. CASH

Before the mid-1965 build-up of American troops in the Vietnam War, it could be said with some degree of certainty that "the night belongs to the Viet Cong." But as the American offensive operations mounted, the enemy could no longer use darkness with impunity.

On any given night in Vietnam, American soldiers staged hundreds of ambushes, for the ambush is one of the oldest and most effective military means of hampering the enemy's night time exploits. Sometimes an ambush was used to provide security for a defensive position or a base camp, sometimes simply to gain information, and at other times to protect villages against enemy terrorists. During the night of 18 June 1967, ten infantrymen of the U.S. 196th Light Infantry Brigade set an ambush at a point sixteen kilometers south of Chu Lai, in Quang Ngai Province, in the hope of waylaying enemy terrorists. (See Map 1 on page 8)

As part of Task Force OREGON, the brigade had been conducting offensive operations to assure the security of the Chu Lai base complex. To this end, the 3d Battalion, 21st infantry, was sending out patrols from a battalion base of operations ten kilometers south of Chu Lai and just north of the Song Tra Bong River, with the specific mission during daylight hours of looking for possible mortar or rocket sites that might pose a threat to the Chu Lai airstrip and at night of establishing ambushes near locations of suspected enemy activity. To accomplish its mission, the ad Battalion had divided its area of responsibility into company sectors, assigning to Company A a sector that included two hamlets, Phuoc An (1) and Phuoc An (2).

When a week's search had uncovered no mortar or rocket sites, the Company A commander decided to establish an ambush in the vicinity of the two hamlets. One of his patrols had heard screams and unusual commotion from one of the hamlets and, later, intelligence reports had indicated that aggressive patrolling just might turn up

Infantryman loading an M79 grenade launcher

something significant. The local Viet Cong, operating in groups of five to twelve men, had been terrorizing villages in the area.

The ambush assignment fell to Company A's 2d Platoon. At 1000 on 18 June the platoon leader, 2d Lt. Truman P. Sullivan, ordered his 2d Squad leader, Sgt. (E-5) Lloyd E. Jones (since it was his turn) to lead the patrol and to use the two fire teams of his own squad. Later, at 1300, he gave the sergeant the details of the mission.

A graduate of the 25th infantry Division Ambush Academy and

considered by many in the battalion a highly professional noncommissioned officer, Sergeant Jones was no stranger to ambushes. He, in turn, named his Fire Team A leader, Sgt. (E-5) Walter R. Nobles, who had been with the brigade since its arrival in Vietnam, as assistant patrol leader. All nine men of Jones's squad were to participate in the action, and for four of them it was to be their first firelight.

From a map study of the co-ordinates designated for the ambush site, Jones determined that the rice paddy terrain in which he would be operating offered no significant tactical advantages to his force. He explained to the patrol members that it was "liable to be," as he put it, "a pretty hairy affair." Simply stated, their mission was to ambush and then capture or kill any enemy moving into the area.

Company standing operating procedure specified equipment to be carried. Each man was to take along four hand grenades. Seven of the fighters were to be armed with M16 rifles, two with M15 rifles that had been issued for test purposes, and two with M79 grenade launchers and pistols. The riflemen would have from 10 to 20 magazines apiece in varying mixes of tracer and ball ammunition, and the grenadiers, in addition to 3 extra pistol magazines, would pack between them 64 high-explosive rounds, 11 canister rounds, and 3 illumination flares. Sergeant Jones elected not to include an M60 machine gun in his arsenal, since three riflemen with ample ammunition, he believed, would provide him with the equivalent firepower without the strain on mobility that a machine gun would impose.

Jones also decided to take along 5 claymore mines, enough, he thought, to cover all trails in the vicinity of the ambush site; 3 smoke grenades; 2 flashlights; and a strobe light. The light was for signalling a medical evacuation helicopter if the need should arise. Spec. 4 Richard A. Jolin, the Team B leader, would carry an unmounted Starlight telescope, a night detection device. Each man would carry water, a first-aid packet, and a small towel for suppressing coughs and sneezes. No food would be taken. Soft caps rather than helmets would be worn. As patrol leader, Jones would have the only map of the area as well as the only compass, along with two star cluster signaling devices. Using a sketch, Jones explained to each man where his position would be and what he was to do. He passed out the patrol's radio frequency and call sign and instructed his men to be ready to move at 1900.

It was 1930 and still daylight when, having cleaned and testified their weapons, the ten infantrymen left the base camp perimeter in a squad column formation, fire teams abreast, Team A on the left and Team B on the right, forty meters apart. Sergeant Jones shot an azimuth with his compass and struck out directly on it for the ambush site, which was in plain view, 1,300 meters away to the southeast. Except for one small creek bed, it was flat open rice paddy all the way, with almost unrestricted observation. Since the dry season had just begun, movement was not difficult.

By 1955 the patrol had reached the staging area that Jones had designated, less than a hundred meters short of the actual site. Since he had never been there before, and because it was the way he operated anyway, Jones moved forward for a better look with his team leaders, Nobles and Jolin, and his radio operator, Spec. 4 Jim Montgomery. What he saw confirmed his map reconnaissance.

It was a clear comfortable night, with the temperature in the mid-seventies, a gentle breeze, and a three-quarter moon. The ambush site the lieutenant had selected was slightly to the northeast of Phuoc An (1) and southwest of Phuoc An (2), in a rice paddy within five hundred meters of each hamlet. A trail connecting the two, with another branch splitting toward the southeast, ran through the paddy. West of the trail was a wood line and farther westward was a slight rise in the ground no more than twenty meters high that ran parallel to the trail. Contiguous to the trail was a trench which appeared not to have been used for some time, a fork of which intersected the trail almost at its juncture point. Underbrush on either side of it partially concealed the trench. The ambush site was also bounded on the south by the trail's south easterly branch. A paddy dike running north to south further defined the location.

To Jones and his assistant, Nobles, the logical spot for the ambush was the trail junction. To avoid having a village at their backs, they chose positions in the northeastern angle of the junction, just inside the rice paddy. Jones positioned his men in four groups, two groups of two men and two of three men.

On the eastern flank he set one of his three-man groups as a security force. It included Jolin, whom he instructed to emplace two claymores along the trail, one covering the village situated to the southeast flank and the other twenty to thirty meters from his position, on the trail. With Jolin were Spec. 4 Victor M. Quinines, armed with an M79

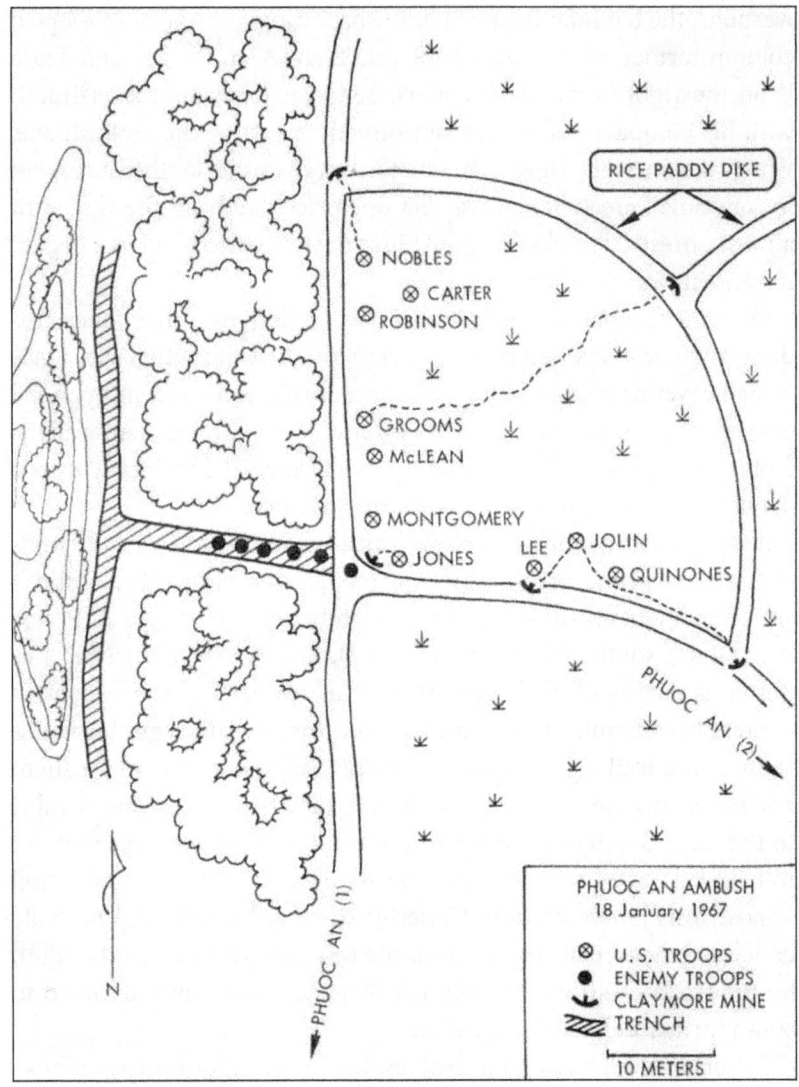

Map 6. Phuoc An Ambush, 18 January 1967

grenade launcher, and Pfc. James H. Lee, who carried an M16 rifle. Jolin had also given the Starlight telescope to Lee, instructing him to check everything around the site in all directions.

Jones placed another three-man security force, commanded by Sergeant Nobles, on the right flank. Nobles set a claymore mine fifteen meters to the right front along the trail to cover his right flank. It was to be used only if the Viet Cong approached from the right, out of the wood line, or from the south on the trail. With Nobles were Pfc. Thomas L. Robinson, armed with an M16 rifle, and Pfc. Douglas G. Carter, a grenadier.

Pfc. Roy J. Grooms and Pfc. Vernon E. McLean, both M16 riflemen, composed the two-man team closest to Nobles' group. Grooms had the additional mission of providing rear security. For this purpose, he controlled a claymore mine, which was emplaced to the rear at the juncture of the two rice paddy dikes.

Sergeant Jones and Specialist Montgomery made up the command group. Both were armed with M16's and Jones had placed a claymore where it could cover most of the trail junction and trench, just two and a half meters away.

By 2010 the ambush party was ready, occupying a position that measured about forty meters from flank to flank with roughly six to eight meters between each group of men. Jones passed the word by radio to company headquarters. (Map 6)

The men had not long to wait. Less than forty-five minutes later Private Lee, scanning westward with his Starlight telescope, detected six men moving single file from the slight rise of ground eastward, directly toward the ambush killing zone. He alerted Jones, who could now see the men walking along in the moonlight, following the edge of the trench. As they continued toward the trail junction, talking and laughing, with no apparent regard for danger, the men in the ambush force tensed for action.

Three of the Viet Cong had already entered the killing zone when the entire group halted. The lead man, who was only a few feet from Sergeant Jones's position, said something and laughed.

Fearing the Viet Cong would detect the ambush, Jones quickly detonated his claymore. In a roar and a boiling cloud of thick, black smoke, the enemy point man disappeared. As the smoke cleared, Jones could see that the explosion had almost torn the man's legs from his body.

While Specialist Montgomery radioed to company headquarters that the ambush had been sprung, the other men in rapid response to the explosion of the claymore opened fire. From the right flank security position, Private Carter fired an M79 canister round at one of the enemy soldiers who, when the claymore exploded, had turned and bolted north along the trail. At a range of twenty meters, Carter missed. As the man disappeared into the wood line, Carter reloaded and fired again, eventually putting about seven rounds into the wood line.

Specialist Quinones, who was one of the eastern flank security force, had his back to the ambush when the firing began. He whirled about, grabbed his grenade launcher, aimed it at the killing zone, and pulled the trigger. Nothing happened. Chagrined, thinking that he had failed to load the weapon during the excitement, he broke it open, verified that the canister round was properly seated, and aimed and fired again—with the same result. This time he reloaded with a fresh canister round and fired at the Viet Cong point man, who, even though he was dying, was trying to inch toward his submachine gun. At a range of only ten meters, Quinones nevertheless missed. The wounded Viet Cong continued to reach for his weapon, finally retrieved it, and was trying to aim it when Montgomery fired an M16 burst into his right side, killing him.

The claymore explosion had also set off enemy fire from the rise of ground not more than twenty-five meters from the trail junction, and a submachine gun was sweeping the trail with sporadic bursts. From the right flank security position, Private Robinson took this weapon under fire with semiautomatic bursts from his M16. In the adjacent two-man team, Private Grooms also fired one round at the Viet Cong machine gun, then followed the lead of Sergeant Nobles and began to throw hand grenades toward the muzzle flash.

Although contact with the enemy had been reported to higher headquarters, neither artillery nor mortar fire was employed. The rules of engagement set by the local village chief, which dictated that no artillery or mortar targets could be taken under fire within 1,000 meters of a hamlet, were firmly applied.

All enemy firing now stopped abruptly. Jones ordered one man of each team to go forward and police up. As Jolin moved toward Jones's position to volunteer to search the enemy dead, a grenade, American or enemy, exploded and a fragment struck him in the right arm. Undeterred, Jolin moved on into the killing zone, where he found Robinson policing the area. A quick search revealed only the gray-cotton uniformed body of the dead Viet Cong point man. Jolin dragged the body into the trench adjacent to the trail and removed a web belt, an M26 fragmentation hand grenade, and a bayonet, all American equipment. Robinson grabbed the enemy weapon, a Chicom 9-mm. submachine gun. Hearing a noise from the wood line next to the trench, Jolin fired a few rounds in that direction with no reaction from the enemy, who apparently had no stomach for continuing the fight. The two soldiers returned to the ambush position.

Mission accomplished, a pleased Sergeant Jones radioed his headquarters that he was coming in. Before leaving, he told Jolin to detonate one claymore and Nobles to blow his. Lest the Viet Cong send reinforcements to the ambush site, Jones pulled back 150 meters across the rice paddies before checking out his men. He then discovered that in addition to Jolin's wound from a grenade fragment, Nobles had taken a small arms round through the right shoulder. The condition of neither man was serious enough to warrant a call for medical evacuation.

The patrol reached the base camp a few moments before midnight. The return trip took much longer because Jones went more slowly on account of the two wounded and used a different route to avoid being ambushed.

Shortly after daylight the next morning the patrol returned to the ambush site, where the men discovered a second body. Further search turned up an American .45-caliber submachine gun and three full magazines, 120 rounds of ammunition, an M14 bayonet, some time fazes, and a Vietnamese-English dictionary. From bloody clothing found at the scene, Jones estimated that the patrol had probably killed two more of the enemy during the exchange.

There was no further sign of the Viet Cong.

4. Fight Along the Rach Ba Rai 15 September 1967

BY JOHN ALBRIGHT

The murmur of voices and the scrape of weapons against the sides of the steel ship penetrated the damp night as the men of the 3d Battalion, 60th Infantry, climbed from a barracks ship, the USS Colleton, and into waiting landing craft alongside. It was 0300, 15 September 1967. Within minutes after boarding the boats, most men slept. Late the previous day they had come back from a three-day operation during which, in one sharp, daylong battle, nine of their comrades had fallen, along with sixty of the enemy. There had been time during the night to clean weapons, shower, eat a hot meal, and receive the new operations order, but not much time to sleep off the now familiar weariness that engulfed these infantrymen after days of fighting both the Viet Cong and the mud of the Mekong Delta.

Three days before Col. Bert A. David's Mobile Riverine Brigade, the 2d Brigade of the 9th Infantry Division, and its Navy counterpart, Task Force 117, had set out to search for and destroy the 514th Local Force and 263d Main Force Viet Cong Battalions. When the enemy was finally found, the ensuing battle had only weakened, not destroyed, the Viet Cong battalions, which broke off the fight and slipped away.

Thus, when intelligence reports that reached the Riverine Brigade's headquarters on the afternoon of 14 September placed the Viet Cong in the Cam Son Secret Zone along the Rach Ba Rai River, Colonel David resolved to attack. (See Map 1 on page 8) Quickly he pulled his units back from the field and into their bases to prepare for a jump-off the next morning. For the 3d Battalion, 60th Infantry, that meant a return to the USS Colleton, anchored in the wide Mekong River near the Mobile Riverine Force's base camp at Dong Tam.

Colonel David planned to trap the Viet Cong in their reported positions along the Rach Ba Rai, a narrow river that flows from the north into the Mekong. (map 7) About ten kilometers north of its confluence with the Mekong, the Rach Ba Rai bends sharply to the

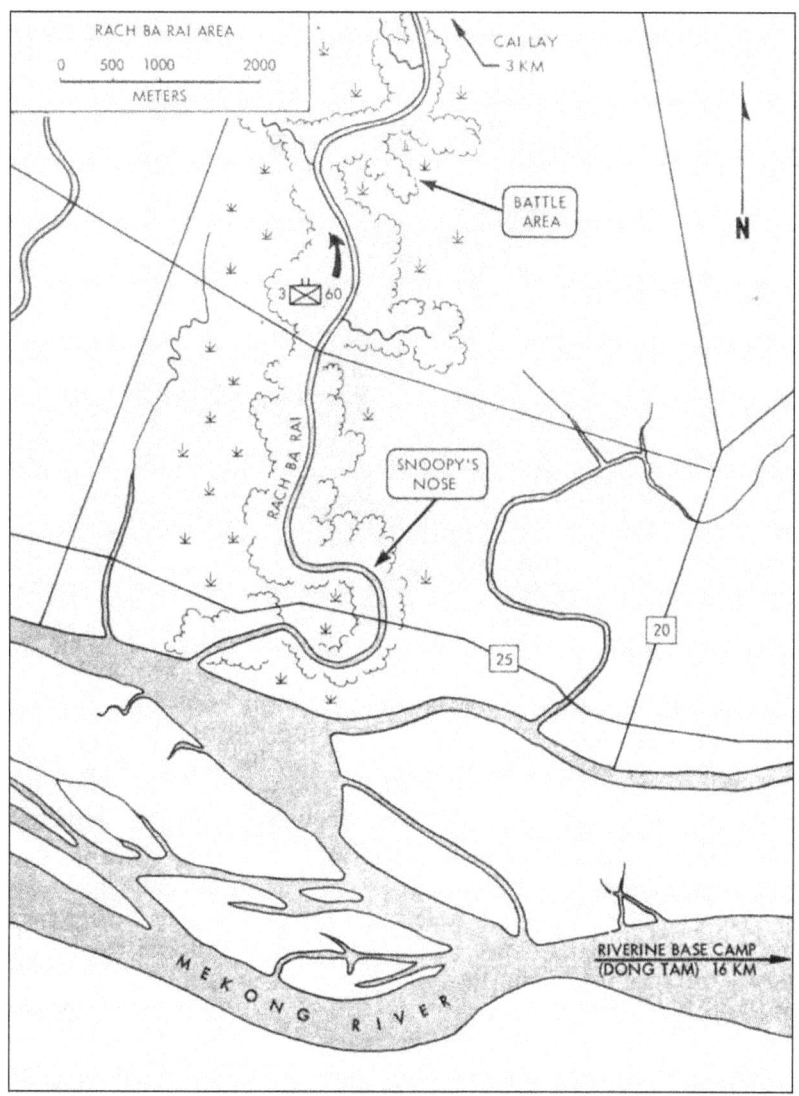

Map 7. Rach Ba Rai area

west for two kilometers, then turns abruptly east for two more before returning to a north-south direction. This bend in the river produces a salient of land that juts to the west, washed on two sides by the river. It was here that the enemy had been reported.

North of the bend, Colonel David planned to emplace the 3d Battalion, 60th Infantry, as a blocking force, but to get to its assigned position the battalion, in Mobile Riverine Force boats, would have to

USS Colleton

sail past the suspected enemy position. South of the bend, Colonel David planned to deploy another blocking force, the 3d Battalion, 47th Infantry. This battalion, also in Riverine Force boats, was to follow the lead unit, the 3d Battalion, 60th Infantry. Together the two battalions would close in on the enemy from the north and south. Once the two infantry battalions had gone ashore in specially modified landing craft known as armored troop carriers (ATC's), the Navy crews were to employ the empty boats as a blocking force. The monitors, gunboats with 20- and 40-mm. guns and 81-mm. direct fire mortars, would reinforce the troop carriers.

While these forces to the north, south, and west formed an anvil, the 5th Battalion, 60th Infantry, advancing overland from the east in M113 armored personnel carriers, would act as a hammer. Other forces could be airlifted into the combat area if needed. Once the enemy troops were trapped, Colonel David planned to destroy them with air strikes and the brigade's three batteries of artillery. The two infantry battalions and the mechanized battalion could then move in and finish the job. Any Viet Cong escaping across the river through the patrolling Navy forces might be intercepted by the South Vietnamese 44th Rangers, operating on an independent mission west of the river.

The commander of the 3d Battalion, 60th Infantry, Lt. Col. Mercer M. Doty, planned to put two of his three companies ashore at the start, Company B on Beach White One and Company A 1,000 meters to the west on Beach White Two. Both units were to land at 0800. Company C (from the 5th Battalion of the 60th Infantry, but under Doty's command) was to stay on the boats as brigade reserve. Traveling in three ATC's, each company was to be reinforced by an engineer squad, a welcome addition since all companies were under strength.

At 0415 the naval convoy transporting the 3d Battalion, 60th Infantry, moved out into the Mekong River preceded by two empty ATC's acting as minesweepers. A monitor gunboat led each of the three groups of armored troop carriers. Interspersed in the column were a helicopter landing deck, medical aid boat and a command and communications boat.

The latter, itself a monitor lacking only the 81-mm. mortar, carried Colonel Doty's staff.

Doty himself circled overhead in his command and control helicopter. Beside him rode Capt. Wayne Jordan, an artillery liaison officer and observer. Lt. Comdr. F. E. ("Dusty") Rhodes, Jr., USN, commanded the boats. Behind the 3d Battalion, 60th Infantry moved the 3d Battalion, 47th Infantry, in basically the same convoy formation.

As the boats churned through the swift Mekong River toward the entrance to the Rach Ba Rai, most of the riflemen in the boats slept while Navy crews manned the guns. On the battalion radio net, routine communications traffic and last-minute planning and coordination messages passed between stations. Among them was a decision to hit Beach White Two at 0730 with a 5-minute artillery preparation, followed by another five minutes' shelling of Beach White One. With only three batteries of artillery available, effective fire could not be laid on both beaches simultaneously.

At 0700 the convoy entered the Rach Ba Rai and headed north, up the narrow channel. Helmets off, flak jackets unzipped, some of the men lay on the troop compartment deck asleep; others rested against the bulkheads, smoking and talking low. On a hunch that the men should be alert, one leader in Company B woke his weapons squad just as the convoy entered the little river. Fifty feet apart, the boats proceeded in a single file, moving about eight miles an hour through the mist of the new morning. Passing a hairpin bend in the river appropriately called "Snoopy's Nose" without incident, they reached the point where the Rach Ba Rai turns west and began to pass the Red Beaches that were to be assaulted by the southern blocking force.

The first warning that something might be amiss came just before 0730. A few rounds of enemy small arms fire kicked up little geysers in the water as the leading boats were nearing the salient of land that was the objective.

Then, precisely at 0730, the sound of an exploding RPG2 antitank rocket split the morning calm, followed almost instantly by a second blast. Minesweeper T-91-4 reeled from the shock of both rockets exploding against its starboard bow. The radios in the boats crackled with the minesweeper's report, "We've been mined." Another boat reported recoilless rifle fire. Seconds later both banks of the thirty-meter-wide stream erupted with fire. Through the din came the unmistakable rip of the AK47 assault rifle and the staccato sound of machine guns.

Radios in the boats came alive with reports. A monitor called, "I'm hit! I hit a mine!" Then came another voice—correctly identifying the blasts—"Somebody's fired a rocket!" Recoilless rifle rounds and rockets, both the RPG2 and the newer, deadlier RPG7, slammed into minesweepers, monitors, and troop-laden ATC's. The roar of dozens of Navy machine guns joined the noise of enemy fire, and as boat after boat entered the ambush and brought more weapons into the fray, 20- and 40-mm. automatic guns and 81-mm. mortars firing point-blank added to the din. Smoke mixed with the morning mist until it became thick, like heavy fog.

Within the first minute, the other ATC that was serving as a minesweeper, T-91-1, took a hit from an RPG2. In the next seven minutes, T-91-1 took four more rockets that wounded eight of its crew. Although ordered to the rear, the boat remained in the battle.

From the Navy radios came a message from Commander Rhodes: "Fire all weapons."

Those boats that had refrained from firing their far-ricocheting .50-caliber machine guns now brought the guns to bear. With their peculiar measured roar, the fifties joined the battle.

As the fighting continued, automatic fire beat against the hulls, some of it coming from bunkers no more than two feet from the water line. For all the counter fire from the boats, antitank rockets and

Armored troop carrier

recoilless rifle rounds kept pouring from mud bunkers on either bank. The heaviest fire came from the east, from an area where intelligence reports had put the Viet Cong. Firing a string of explosive 40-mm. rounds into the aperture of one bunker on the east bank, a Navy gunner blew the top off the fortification and silenced it. Although most enemy positions were within five meters of the water and formed a killing zone 1,500 meters long, few of the Army troops saw much more of the enemy than his gun flashes.

As the line of boats moved deeper into the ambush, the intensity of the fight grew. Some boats slowed while others speeded up, but all poured fire from every operable gun. As fast as they could, the gunners fired, reloaded, and fired again.

After only a few moments of letting the Navy do the fighting, the troops joined in with M79 grenade launchers, M60 machine guns, and M16 rifles. The men climbed, crawled, or ran to firing positions while officers saw to it that machine gunners and M79 grenadiers got the better locations.

In the first flush of the engagement, many of the Navy weapons momentarily fell silent, their crews wounded or killed. Acting

Monitor

sometimes under orders from company officers, but in most cases on their own, soldiers took over Navy guns so that few weapons went long unused, even though casualties constantly mounted.

Commanding the 3d Platoon of Company B, 3d Battalion, 60th Regiment, 1st Lt. Peter M. Rogers saw six of his men hit in the first few seconds. Many of the Navy crewmen on Rogers' boat also were hit and riflemen quickly took their places. When the company commander, Capt. Wilbert Davis, took hold of a Navy machine gun to return fire, one of his platoon sergeants moved in to relieve him, only to take an enemy bullet in the chest. As the sergeant fell to the deck another man quickly took the gun.

Running from the main deck to the gun turret in search of a better view of the enemy positions, Capt. Gregg R. Orth, commanding Company A, took over an unmanned machine gun and opened fire. When the gun malfunctioned, he ran below decks, found a machine gunner, and sent him up to fix it. Just then he noted that the two Navy machine guns at the bow had quit firing. Surmising that they had malfunctioned, he sent two of Company A's machine gunners to remove the Navy weapons and replace them with two of the company's

M60's.

Sgt. John L. White of Company B, spotting a man in a tree, turned to a nearby machine gunner shouting, "There's a sniper in the tree!" The gunner fired a long burst from his M60 and set the tree ablaze. As the two men scanned the area for another target, the blast from an exploding rocket knocked both of them down, but seconds later they were on their feet and firing.

So fast and sustained was the fire from the American weapons that at least two M60 machine gun barrels burned out. To help the M79 gunners, other soldiers knelt by the bow, ripping open cases of ammunition. On one boat alone, three M79 gunners disposed of three cases of ammunition in twenty minutes.

With only sporadic breaks, the battle continued. Round after round struck both troop carriers and monitors. The boats veered right and left in the narrow channel, some jockeying for position, some temporarily out of control as coxswains were wounded. The blast from a rocket explosion knocked one boat commander off his feet and under a .50-caliber gun tub. Although stunned, he made it back to the wheel a minute later, but in the meantime the boat had careened dangerously.

Three minutes after the fight started a monitor, 111-2, took two RPG2 rounds, one in the cockpit that shot away the steering mechanism. The boat captain managed to beach the monitor while crewmen worked frantically to repair the damage. The job done quickly, 111-2 lunged again into midstream.

At the same time that the monitor was hit, the command and communications boat took two antitank rockets on the port 40-mm. gun mount. Although the rounds did no damage, they served to acquaint the battalion staff fully with the nature of the situation. A few minutes later, the command boat took another hit. This round knocked Commander Rhodes unconscious, but a few seconds later he was back on his feet.

To the men in the troop carriers it appeared that the Viet Cong were trying to hit the frames holding the canvas sun cover over the troop compartment and rain down fragments on the closely bunched men below. Most of the rounds that seemed to be aimed that way sailed harmlessly over the boats, for such shooting demanded the best marksmanship or incredible luck. The few rockets that struck the metal frames wounded scores of men, in one case killing one and wounding almost every other man in a platoon of Company B.

However fierce the enemy fire, both the Army and Navy radios went on operating. Amid messages asking' for the medical aid boat and questions as to whether any "friendlier" were ashore (the men were concerned lest they fire into their own troops), fragmentary reports on the battle flashed back to the command and communications boat and from there back to brigade headquarters.

Word of the ambush reached the brigade operations officer, Maj. Johnnie H. Corns, who was monitoring the progress of the convoy, about three minutes after the fight began. The first report had it that two of the boats were on fire. With the concurrence of the brigade commander, Colonel David, Major Corns directed that the 3d Battalion, 47th Infantry, be prepared to assume the mission of Colonel Doty's battalion—landing on Beach White One and Two. If that turned out to be necessary, the 3d Battalion, 60th Infantry, would land south of the bend, close to the beaches previously given the name of Beach Red One and Two.

Flying above the action in his helicopter, the commander of the 3d Battalion, 60th Infantry, Colonel Doty, also listened to the first reports of the fighting. His first reaction was a wry satisfaction that at least the enemy was where they had expected him to be. It was all the more important now, Doty believed, to proceed with the operation as planned, to run the gauntlet and get the men ashore on Beach White One and Two.

Artillery observers flying overhead in spotter aircraft called in fire on the Viet Cong positions minutes after the first enemy round crashed into the lead minesweeper. Two batteries of 105-mm. howitzers, B and C of the 3d Battalion, 34th Artillery, fired from support positions south of the battle site, while Battery A, 1st Battalion, 27th Artillery, reinforced their fires from a support base to the northeast. Although they cut down the volume of enemy fire, three batteries could not cope with all the enemy fire coming from an ambush site 1,500 meters long. The 105's could deal effectively with spider holes and other open firing positions, but a direct hit from a piece as heavy as a 155 was needed to knock out a bunker.

At 0735, Monitor 111-3 was hit by two RPG2's. The first knocked out the main gun, the 40-mm. encased in a turret, killing the Navy gunner and wounding two other seamen. The second wounded three

Navy machine gunner of the Riverine Force

more crewmen. Two minutes later a third antitank rocket smashed into the 81-mm. mortar pit, wounding two marines and a sailor, but the monitor stayed in the fight.

Elsewhere many of the direct hits by RPG2's did little damage. Each of the boats carrying platoons of Capt. Richard E. Botelho's Company C, for example, took at least one rocket hit, but no crewmen or soldiers were injured. Botelho was grateful for the fact that the Viet Cong were "lousy shots." Few of the thousands of enemy bullets pierced the armor of the boats. On the other hand, few of the American rounds were able to penetrate the enemy's bunkers. The Navy's 81-mm. mortar shells and 40-mm. high-explosive rounds would knock out enemy bunkers only when they passed through the firing slits. Yet however ineffective in killing the foe, each side maintained a steady fire, for one side to lessen the volume was to give the other side an opportunity to aim more precisely and bring all its weapons to bear. So close were some of the enemy's positions to the water line that some of the Navy guns were unable to depress low enough to hit them. Only when the men on the boats were able to catch the Viet Cong popping up from their spider holes or from behind mounds of earth could they deal with them effectively.

Within five to ten minutes after the ambush was sprung, the forward motion of the convoy ceased, but individual boats darted back and forth, continually passing each other, some keeping to midstream, others making passes toward the bank before veering off, their machine guns and heavy weapons in action all the while. One boat sped past the momentarily crippled Monitor 111-3, possibly trying to protect it. Just beyond the monitor, the boat shuddered under the blows of four or five rockets, but its fire never stopped. Another monitor, temporarily out of control, brushed the east bank but moments later Swung back into midstream and into the fight.

Colonel Doty still was convinced that his troops could break through the ambush and land according to plan. He saw that the channel was filled with twisting, weaving boats, was laced with fire, and was far too narrow to pass the 3d Battalion, 47th Infantry, through while the fight was on. Then, as Doty watched, a single boat broke out of the killing zone and headed toward the White Beaches. Encouraged by this breakthrough, the colonel ordered his S-3, Maj. Richard H. Sharp, to "send in the troops." As Davis' boat made its dash for the beach, Colonel Doty in the helicopter above decided to make the run with him. At this point the boat took a rocket hit on the "Boston whaler" lashed to its deck. The little skiff shattered, but its outboard motor soared high in the air, and, as Doty followed its course, plummeted into the river, where it landed with a mighty splash.

By the time Major Sharp acknowledged the call and relayed the order to the lead company commander, Captain Davis could reply: "Roger, I have one element ashore now, waiting for the rest." For all the intensity of the enemy fire, Davis' boat, with Company B's command group and one platoon aboard had broken through.

The rest of the boats, nevertheless, remained embroiled in the fight. At 0745, Monitor 111-3 took an RPG2 round on its portside that burned a hole completely through the armor and wounded one man. At about the same time, ATC 111-6 reeled under the impact of two antitank rounds but no one was hurt and the boat's fire continued unabated. A third round hit the .50-caliber mount a minute later, killing a Navy crewman and wounding five more. At this point Commander Rhodes decided that the fire was too heavy and the danger of mines—now that the minesweepers were partially disabled—was too great to justify continuing to run the gauntlet. In fact, Navy Riverine standing operating procedure required that troop carriers be preceded by minesweepers. Moreover, he urgently needed replacement crews. At 0750, twenty minutes after the battle began, Rhodes therefore ordered all boats to turn back. They were to assemble downstream in the vicinity of the Red Beaches on the south side of the bend.

The withdrawal, under intense fire, began immediately. All the while artillery still rained on the enemy and the boats continued their fire as long as they remained in range. Four Air Force A-37's, earlier scheduled to strike the White Beaches under the original plan, roared in to put bombs and napalm on the Viet Cong positions. The enemy also continued to fire; in one case two rockets came so close to the RC-292 antennas on the command and communications boat that the rocket fins severed the lead-in wires.

One by one the boats broke out of the killing zone and headed for Beach Red Two. There the aid boat became a magnet as all boat commanders concentrated on getting help for their wounded.

Until the Navy task group commander ordered the withdrawal, Colonel Doty and his S-3 had continued to urge the remainder of Company B to pass through the ambush and join Captain Davis and his single platoon at Beach White One. At 0802, when Doty heard of the withdrawal order, he had no choice but to comply. He ordered Davis and his little band on the beach to re-embark and run the gauntlet in reverse.

Engaged by the enemy on the beach, Captain Davis and the platoon began to withdraw a few yards at a time. Putting up a heavy fire to the front, they ran in twos and threes back into ATC 111-6. When all were safely on board, Davis called the battalion S-3 and reported laconically, "We're coming back now." Raising the ramp, the boat captain backed into the stream, brought the bow around slowly, and, gunning the engines to full speed, called out to Davis, "I'll get you through, Captain." Riding with the current, the craft began to run the gauntlet, a lone boat with about thirty men, proceeding again through the fire of the Viet Cong.

Rockets and bullets rained on the boat, but incredibly only one struck a telling blow. The craft was halfway through the ambush when a rocket hit the port .50-caliber mount. One sailor fell, killed instantly, and four of his comrades were wounded. But from that point the troop carrier made it safely back to the Red Beach assembly area.

At Red Beach Capt. James H. Bledsoe, the battalion's S-4, who rode with the command group, was organizing resupply and medical evacuation for the wounded. An occasional sniper round whizzed through the area, though without effect, as boat after boat made its way to transfer the few dead and many wounded to the aid boat. There the battalion chaplain, Capt. James D. Johnson, and the surgeon, Capt. Charles Hughes, ministered to the wounded. Minor fires burned on two boats, one in a box of equipment, the other in a Boston whaler. As the crews fought the fires, other boats came alongside to assist. Thanks to Bledsoe's efforts, by 0844 medical evacuation helicopters began to land on the deck of the aid boat to take the seriously wounded back to the base hospital at Dong Tam. Of the scores wounded, only twenty-four required evacuation.

Boats carrying platoons of the same company began to gather together. Platoon leaders scrambled into the company headquarters boats to brief their commanders, while the men worked to redistribute ammunition, replace damaged machine gun barrels, and radio back to the Mobile Riverine base for resupply by helicopter. Calling back to Navy headquarters, Commander Rhodes requested two minesweepers and a monitor from the force transporting the 3d Battalion, 47th Infantry—now halted a few thousand meters downstream—to replace his three most badly damaged boats. Every one of his monitors and minesweepers, Rhodes reported, had been hit.

His troops out of the ambush and reorganizing smoothly, Colonel Doty directed his helicopter to a nearby fire support base to refuel. While on the ground, he conferred with Brig. Gen. William B. Fulton, one of the assistant 9th Infantry Division commanders. Getting ashore on the White Beaches, Fulton said, was the most critical element in the plan. Colonel Doty was confident that the boats with his men aboard could get past the Viet Cong and go ashore.

Returning to the air, Doty radioed the brigade commander, recommending that the battalion try again to get through. Colonel David agreed and ordered Doty to try it as soon as the Navy task group was ready.

Resupply of boats and men meanwhile proceeded swiftly. By 0900 two replacement minesweepers and a replacement monitor had arrived among the boats transporting the 3d Battalion, 47th Infantry. The boats also brought replacements for many of the Navy wounded, so that the Navy crews soon were close to full strength.

For the second attempt to run the ambush and get ashore on the White Beaches, Colonel Doty directed that Captain Botelho's Company C replace Davis' Company B. which as the lead company had been hit the hardest in the first try. Company B would serve as the brigade's ready reaction force. To support the fresh effort, a light fire team of two armed Huey helicopters arrived overhead. Doty arranged for the artillery to begin firing as the task force neared the southern edge of the ambush zone and then to walk its fires up both banks of the river just ahead of the boats as the convoy sailed northward. Both soldiers and sailors were to "reconnoitre by fire" against the banks, but because American troops were moving overland to hit the enemy from the east, the 20- and 40-mm. guns and .50-caliber machine guns were to be used only against the west bank.

While the boats were still forming for the second try, the first of sixteen air strikes ordered for the rest of the day began. Three F-4C Phantom jets—their shrill, whistling scream preceding them— came in to drop bombs and napalm on the middle of the ambush zone, a hundred meters inland from the east bank.

Just after 1000 the second attempt to run through the enemy force began. This time no element of surprise existed for either side; the issue would be settled by firepower alone. But the Americans now possessed considerably more firepower. In addition to the three batteries of artillery walking shells up the banks, the helicopter gunships and the jets would add their fire. Their combined fires were expected to keep the enemy from effectively engaging the passing boats.

The convoy entered the ambush zone with every weapon in action, aided by the helicopters and artillery. Yet again the enemy opened fire, and the fight raged all along the ambush line. If any of the Viet Cong had withdrawn it failed to show in the volume of firepower. From the earth-covered bunkers, heavy weapons fire poured onto the boats, but they kept moving up the river. As in the earlier run, one of the two lead minesweepers was hit first: T-91-3 took two rockets, one in the coxswain's flat, one on the port .50-caliber mount. Then an ATC was hit and five of the replacement crew were wounded. Again a small boat atop the troop carrier caught fire. Although the other minesweeper was hit seven times by rockets, only three of the crew were wounded.

Rocket after rocket passed inches over the tops of the crew

compartments of the ATC's, the men inside certain that the Viet Cong gunners were trying again to explode their rockets so that they would scatter deadly fragments into the troop compartments. Again, in one case, they succeeded. A rocket detonated against the starboard canopy of ATC 111-10, spewing fragments on the men below. Two Navy crewmen and eighteen soldiers were wounded. Miraculously, only one soldier died. In one blow, Company A's ad Platoon was struck down; only five men of the platoon would leave the boat to fight on the beach.

The first boats reached White Beach Two and the Navy crews were soon nosing their craft against the muddy banks. As they dropped their ramps, the men of Companies A and C dashed ashore, followed shortly by Company B as the brigade commander released the company from its role as reserve.

Hardly had the men landed and run a few feet in from the river when fire from individual Viet Cong riflemen began to fall among them, punctuated at a few points by automatic weapons fire. The troops returned the fire, relying chiefly on M79 grenade launchers with canister ammunition. As the men hugged the ground, artillery shells fell ahead of them, stopping only when three F-100's roared in to drop bombs and napalm a short distance in front. Then a second flight of two F-100's followed to drop bombs and strafe with 20-mm. guns. Once the aircraft had finished their run, the artillery quickly returned to the fight.

The three company commanders meanwhile checked by radio to determine the losses incurred in running upriver. Companies B and C had made the passage with only a few men slightly wounded. Since Company A, the hardest hit, had lost eighteen men wounded in one platoon alone, Captain Orth expressed doubt to Colonel Daly that his command could accomplish its mission. Doty replied: "You haven't got much choice; you've got to continue on." Orth answered, "We're moving out."

The biggest problem the troops on shore faced at the moment was a lack of visibility. They could see neither the enemy that occasionally taunted them with fire nor many of their own number, for soon after leaving the river bank they were swallowed up by dense scrub jungle. The thick foliage also prevented supporting fire from those Navy boats that had stayed behind from the mission of patrolling the river

Helicopter landing deck medical aid boat

in order to aid the ground troops; gunners on the boats could not see the troops. Although the companies were within 150 meters of each other, an hour passed before all three had established physical contact. Meanwhile, the companies cleared drop zones to facilitate aerial resupply and evacuation of the wounded.

Overhead, Colonel Doty observed artillery fire, coordinated air strikes, and assisted his companies in linking up. Around noon, as the companies at last had established contact, he received a message from brigade headquarters directing a change in mission. Instead of serving as a blocking force while the 5th Battalion, 60th Infantry, moved overland from the east, the 3d Battalion, 60th Infantry, was to drive south while the 3d Battalion, 47th Infantry, after landing on the Red Beaches, pushed north. The 5th Battalion, 60th Infantry, mission to push west remained, but the battalion was to be augmented by the 2d Battalion, 60th Infantry, brought in by helicopter. Thus four battalions would press against the enemy from three sides.

About 200 meters from the river, the men at last emerged into more open terrain, Company C on the left in a field of high grass and cane and Company A on the right in a dry rice paddy. Yet leaving the jungle behind was a mixed blessing, for the enemy immediately

Command and communications boat

raked the fields with small arms and automatic weapons fire. As the men hit the ground, few had any idea where the elusive enemy was hidden. Most were content to hold their fire while forward observers with the company commanders called in support. The artillery did the job. When the fire stopped the companies resumed their advance. Although some of the men in Companies A and B could see each other now, Company C was still lost from view.

Passing through a wood line that had only moments before sheltered the enemy, Company A's forward observer saw three of the Viet Cong run into a cluster of huts ("hootches," the men called them). As infantrymen fired M79's against the huts, the forward observer called in artillery.

At about the same time, Spec. 4 David H. Hershberger, a machine gunner in Company A, spotted one of the Viet Cong, brought his heavy weapon to his shoulder, and dropped the man with a short burst. When a second enemy soldier popped up from the ground and ran toward his downed partner, Hershberger shouted, "There's another one," grabbed an M14 from a sniper-trained rifleman, and dropped the second man with one round at about 250 meters.

Slowly, for much of the rest of the afternoon, the southward advance continued. From time to time enemy fire increased sharply, forcing the infantry to cover, but air strikes, artillery, and the riflemen's determination to move ahead kept the advance going. As the afternoon waned, the battalion was nevertheless only about 500 meters south of Beach White Two. When at 1700 Colonel Doty reported to brigade that his units were heavily engaged, Colonel David deemed it better to risk the Viet Cong's escaping than to have the troops face the night disorganized. He instructed Colonel Doty to break contact and pull back into a night defensive position. Leaving patrols behind to cover the withdrawal, the companies pulled back to a position near Beach White Two, in the process eliminating bypassed snipers as they went.

By late afternoon the companies had linked in a semicircular night defensive position with the river and the Navy boats at their backs. Captain Davis, the senior company commander, took charge. As darkness fell, even sporadic sniper fire ceased. Through the night the command stood at 50 percent alert, a Spooky flare and gunship overhead kept the area constantly illuminated and artillery dropped on suspected enemy locations. The enemy made no effort to penetrate the perimeter, and the next morning the reason became apparent. He was less interested in fighting than in slipping out of the closing trap.

That many of the Viet Cong succeeded in escaping became clear as patrols of converging battalions, moving against only infrequent rifle fire, established contact. The rest of the morning the men checked approximately 250 enemy bunkers, discovering 79 enemy bodies, victims of small arms fire, artillery, and air strikes. Presumably, many more of the enemy had been wounded. The American forces, all four battalions and the Navy crews, had a total of only 7 killed. But the fighting had exacted a toll of 123 wounded. Many had not required evacuation, however. Four of the enemy were detained, and one surrendered under the Chieu Hoi ("Open Arms") program, using a safe conduct pass picked up in the area.

From the first shot of the ambush, the fighting had been almost continuous, and much of the time heavy. Both sides had been hurt, the 263d Main Force Viet Cong Battalion by far the worst. Though it had left the field badly mauled, it was by no means destroyed.

The 3d Battalion, 60th Infantry, and the 263d Viet Cong Battalion would meet again.

5. Three Companies at Dak To 6 November 1967

BY ALLAN W. SANDSTRUM

In early February 1954, French Union forces were drawn into the final, convulsive combat actions of the Indochina War. A closing act of that drama took place on 2 February when the Viet Minh launched simultaneous attacks in battalion strength that overwhelmed all French outposts northwest of Kontum City. By 7 February the French high command, realizing that its tenuous hold on Kontum Province had been broken, evacuated the provincial capital. The ejection of French forces from this key province in the Central Highlands marked a giant step in the march of Communist insurgency.

Thirteen years later, reconstituted Communist forces readied another major effort in Kontum Province. Although the stage was the same, the cast and scale of confrontation were somewhat different. This time regular units of the North Vietnamese Army (NVA) prepared to strike a telling blow against South Vietnamese and U.S. Military Assistance Command forces. The North Vietnamese Army objective was not to reduce all Free World outposts in Kontum, but to chalk up a sorely needed victory by seizing just one—the Dak To complex—a few kilometers from a key French post of the same name that was overrun in 1954.

Dak To was one of a chain of Civilian Irregular Defense Group (CIDG) camps advised by U.S. Special Forces personnel. Situated in the west central part of Kontum Province, it could be reached from Pleiku City by following Route 14 north through Kontum City and then turning west on Route 512. North of Dak To, Route 14 rapidly deteriorated as it approached a CIDG camp at Dak Seang. Still farther to the north the road became so poor that another camp at Dak Pek had to rely solely on an aerial life line. (Map 8)

During 1967 each of the CIDG camps in western Kontum had been threatened by North Vietnamese forces on one or more occasions. The ultimate security of these isolated garrisons was the responsibility

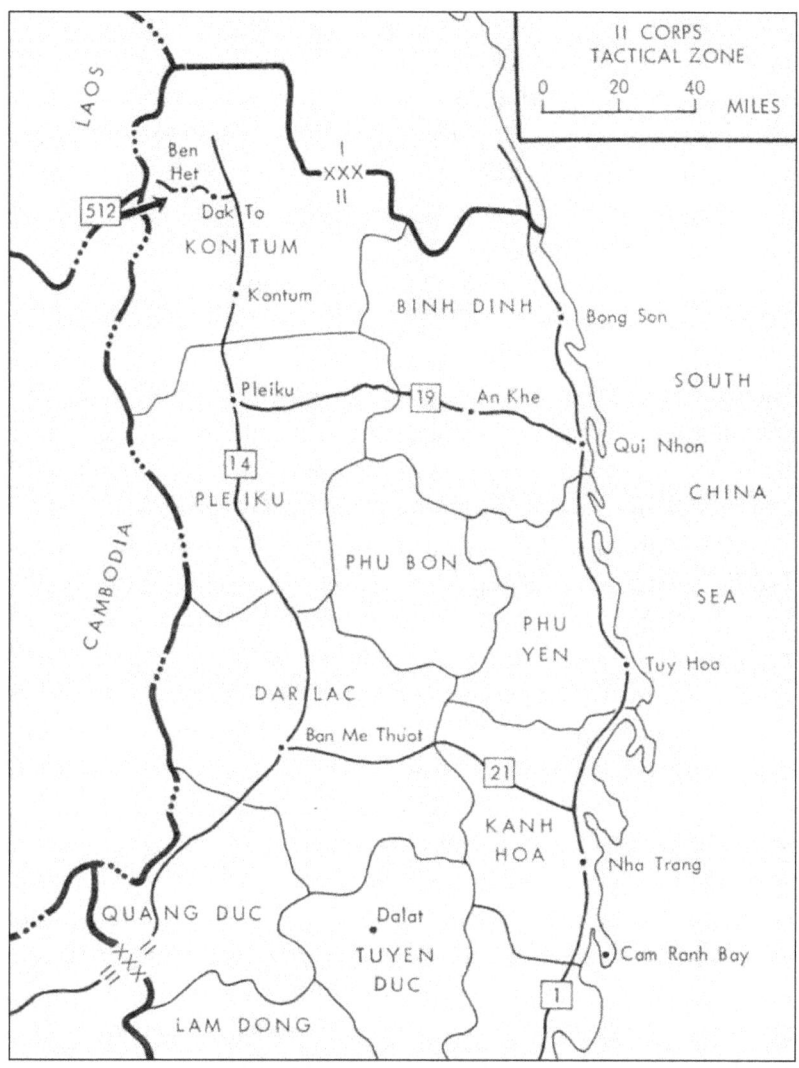

Map 8. II Corps, tactical zone

of the U.S. 4th Infantry Division, whose area of operations was so extensive as to include most of Kontum and Pleiku Provinces and the northern part of Darlac Province. In early October 1967 the 4th Division was screening Kontum with one mechanized battalion.

Late in October gleanings from bits and pieces of intelligence gave solid indications that the W3 Front—control headquarters for North Vietnamese Army operations in the Central Highlands—was moving the bulk of its regiments from bases along the Cambodian border and other remote areas of the highlands into Kontum Province under the control of the NVA 1st Division. Since most of the elements of that division operated in Pleiku Province and the south western panhandle of Kontum Province, their presence in central Kontum represented a shift of from sixty to a hundred kilometers to the north. Thus warned that the NVA 1st Division was preparing its battlefield, U.S. forces began swift counter preparations.

On 28 October the 4th Infantry Division replaced the mechanized battalion with the 3d Battalion, 12th Infantry. Pushing out long-range reconnaissance patrols, the 3d Battalion immediately detected enemy movement from the southwest toward Dak To. Agent reports corroborated this finding. The attention of the division and its senior headquarters, I Field Force, Vietnam, was now riveted on what appeared to be a developing storm. (See Map 1 on page 8)

On 29 October the 4th Division moved its 1st Brigade headquarters to Dak To and on the following day strengthened its forces in the vicinity with the 3d Battalion, 8th Infantry. Intensified enemy patrolling, the findings of sensitive airborne personnel detectors, and the discovery of several recently established base camps and ammunition caches indicated a large enemy build-up. The NVA 1st Division, however, was apparently still unprepared to make its thrust.

Lt. Gen. William B. Rosson, commanding U.S. I Field Force, further strengthened his troops in Kontum when, on 1 November, he drew the 4th Battalion, 503d Infantry, from the operational control of the 173d Airborne Brigade and airlifted it from Phu Yen Province to Dak To. At that point three U.S. battalions were in position. It was the second foray into Kontum for men of the 173d Airborne Brigade. During the previous summer they had fought a series of bloody actions against regular North Vietnamese units south of Dak To.

Additional information about enemy strength, composition, and disposition continued to accumulate during the next twenty-four hours. On 2 November Sgt. Vu Hong slipped away from a reconnaissance party of the NVA 66th Regiment and surrendered at the village of Bak Ri near Route 512. His fifty-man group had been selecting firing positions for mortars and 122-mm. rocket launchers. He declared that his own regiment and four others he identified were converging on Dak To and a new CIDG camp under construction at Ben Het, eighteen kilometers west of Dak To.

Lt. Col. James H. Johnson, commander of the 4th Battalion, 503d Infantry, was ordered on 2 November to meet the enemy threat west of Dak To. That afternoon he sent his Company C to Ben Het by road, and the next day he followed with the rest of his battalion. There, amid a clutter of engineer equipment being used to construct the CIDG camp, he began to establish a fire support base.

The two battalions of the 4th Division had meanwhile deployed to high ground south and southwest of Dak To. Elements of these battalions drew first blood in separate encounters with elements of the NVA 32d Regiment on 3 and 4 November. In each fight U.S. casualties were comparatively light because supporting fires played a major role. Artillery and air strikes blasted enemy forces who occupied strong defensive positions south of the Dak To Special Forces Camp.

Judging from these first encounters, the enemy had altered his plans in response to the rapid build-up of American forces and had retired to carefully prepared defensive positions. From these positions, intelligence analysts conjectured, the North Vietnamese intended to await an attack and then attempt to maul American and South Vietnamese forces. This hypothesis could soon be tested further, for the NVA 66th Regiment had already occupied the high ground southwest of Ben Het. Regardless of the risks involved in attacking the enemy on terrain of his choosing, the rare opportunity to catch the North Vietnamese in any concentration of forces could not be passed up.

Colonel Johnson believed that his battalion would first come to grips with the enemy in or near a small valley approximately seven kilometers southwest of the new fire support base at Ben Het. Holding back Company B to secure and help construct the base, he immediately pushed Companies A, C, and D on roughly parallel axes to the south and southwest. He told his company commanders that somewhere in front of them up to two North Vietnamese battalions were waiting.

The first day of the operation was without incident. It was apparent that for the moment Dak To was not menaced by ground attack from the west. The three companies at first pursued divergent paths so that their night positions were approximately 1,600 meters apart—Company D in the center, Company C to the west, and Company A to the east.

Unlike the others in this typical airborne battalion, Company D was

Laden soldiers pushing through elephant grass near Dak To

a provisional force, created by taking men from various other units of the battalion. The company had only three officers and eighty-five men, organized in two instead of the usual four platoons. Lacking a weapons platoon, the company had six M60 ma chine gun crews, one with each rifle squad Company D had no mortars or recoilless rifles.

For all the company's provisional nature and the men's status as paratroopers, on this mission the troops operated much as did any American infantrymen in Vietnam, even to the amount and variety of weapons and equipment they carried. Each man bore a rucksack that weighed up to fifty pounds. Strapped, lashed, or otherwise attached to his perspiring frame, a typical rifleman was laden with three days' rations, 500 rounds of M16 rifle ammunition (often carried in a discarded claymore bag), 4 fragmentation and 2 smoke grenades, 200 M60 machine gun rounds, and 3 canteens of water. In his hands he clutched his basic weapon, the fully automatic M16 rifle, ready for instant use.

Bronzed mountain men marched with the Americans: a platoon-size Civilian Irregular Defense Group force, based at the Dak To Special Forces Camp, was attached to each company. Master Sergeant Ky, Vietnamese Special Forces, led the thirty-man Montagnard platoon attached to Company D.

These small, wiry irregulars carried a hodgepodge of weapons—M1 rifles, carbines, Browning automatic rifles, and submachine guns—all of U.S. manufacture.

On 4 November the axis of the three companies reached their maximum divergence. Reacting to 4th Division intelligence that the headquarters of the NVA 40th Artillery Regiment was then located five kilometers southeast of Ben Het, Johnson ordered Capt. James J. Muldoon to change Company A's direction temporarily and search the suspected area. About 1300 Muldoon's men turned eastward and marched until 2000. That night the three companies were 1,800 to 2,200 meters apart. It had been another day without incident. Thus far the only enemy force threatening Dak To was engaged with the two battalions of the 4th Infantry Division, south and southwest of the camp.

On the morning of the 5th, still finding no trace of the enemy, Muldoon and Company A began moving back again toward the southwest. As the result of a discussion with Colonel Johnson, Muldoon was now to trail Company D instead of resuming his march on Company D's left flank. From such a position his force would be more readily available as a reserve. A hard march faced Muldoon's men as they labored to narrow the gap. They were not to encamp until

97

1600.

Company C came upon the trail of the North Vietnamese that day at 1130, five kilometers from the fire support base. The first of the three companies to ascend the higher ground of the Ngok Kom Leat mountain complex, Company C discovered some unoccupied enemy foxholes. Less than an hour later the company found another group of foxholes 500 meters to the south.

The distance between the companies and their Ben Het base was lengthening. Col. Richard H. Johnson, commanding the 1st Brigade, directed Lt. Col. James H. Johnson (the battalion commander) to establish a new fire support base closer to the anticipated area of combat. After making an aerial reconnaissance together, they selected Hill 823 because it dominated the terrain and would be mutually supporting with Ben Het. Relieved of the mission of providing security for Ben Het, Company B was to conduct an air assault onto the hill at 0900 on the following day, 6 November. Companies A, C, and D were directed to link up at the new base.

On 6 November the airborne soldiers march to combat gathered momentum. For the men trudging through tangled Kontum forests, it was the fourth day on the trail.

Only Company A was slow to clear its night camp site. The pace of the previous day had been intense, and weary troopers had been forced to hack out a landing zone for the regular evening aerial resupply—an operation carried over to the next morning. When the men finally moved out in column around 0900, they made rapid progress in closing the gap between themselves and Company D. S. Sgt. David Terrazas and his squad remained at the camp site as a rear guard. An hour after the departure of the main body, they slipped away to rejoin the column.

Approximately 1,500 meters ahead of Company A, Capt. Thomas H. Baird's Company D was already well clear of its night position. The company moved south, down from high ground into a valley, then shifted toward the southwest and west, seeking greater ease of movement on the lower ridgelines of Ngok Kom Leat.

Spec. 4 Emory L. Jorgensen, the point man, spotted it first—communications wire, beckoning enticingly up a trail. It was 1130. A quick reconnaissance along 200 meters of the wire uncovered nothing more than an uncommunicative white pith helmet. The wire ran west,

Montagnard irregulars

pointing toward the higher reaches of the ridge.

Captain Baird asked permission to divert his company from its mission long enough to follow the wire to its terminus. From a command helicopter overhead, Colonel Johnson granted the request. Baird settled his men into a perimeter, then, with artillery support, he sent two squads to conduct a cloverleaf sweep on each side of the trail. The searchers found no further sign of the enemy and at 1230 re-entered the company position.

The captain then moved his company up the trail, his four-man point element followed by the 2d Platoon, the Montagnard irregulars and the 1st Platoon. As time edged toward 1300, the point reported that the trail was widening perceptibly as it ascended the ridgeline, approaching an intermediate knoll 100 meters away. (Map 9)

A feeling of tense expectation that already permeated the column heightened as the men reached the knoll. Fresh prints of bare feet in the soft ground, a bamboo reel for wire, newly dropped human faeces—all pointed to the nearness of the enemy. Baird first drew his force into a defensive perimeter, then began to advance by bounds, at each halt sending four squads out on cloverleaf sweeps in an effort to circumvent any possible enemy ambush. 1st Lt. Michael D. Burton, 2d Platoon, sent his two lead squads forward to conduct the initial sweep up the ridge. As S. Sgt. Jimmy R. Worley's 1st Squad began to move out of the 2d Platoon defensive position, the hair raising chatter of automatic weapons fire sounded from less than fifty meters up the hill.

In an instant, four days of dogged slogging in search of the enemy were forgotten in the shock of combat.

Lieutenant Burton pulled his 1st Squad back, then sent it around to the left flank and up the ridge again. From the right, the 2d Squad supported the move, attempting to suppress enemy fire with its M60 machine gun and M79 grenade launcher. As the 1st Squad moved up the hill in an attempt to flank enemy gunners, it came upon a small clearing. There Spec. 4 Charles E. Moss spotted a green-uniformed North Vietnamese soldier carrying an AK47. When the man turned away, Moss cut him down with a short burst from his M16. A fire fight ensued.

Baird then ordered Burton to pull his platoon back along the trail into a company perimeter. To disengage would not be an easy matter but it was preferable to the possible piecemeal destruction of a company strung out in column. While Worley's men fell back, the 2d and 3d Squads continued to lay down covering fire. As if on cue, intense automatic weapons fire from up the trail rained down on the 2d Squad and spilled over into the company position. Two assistant M60 gunners and a rifleman were wounded. Subsequent events crowded together with lightning rapidity.

Although the company for the moment still lacked its engaged 2d Platoon, other elements were forming a defensive position with

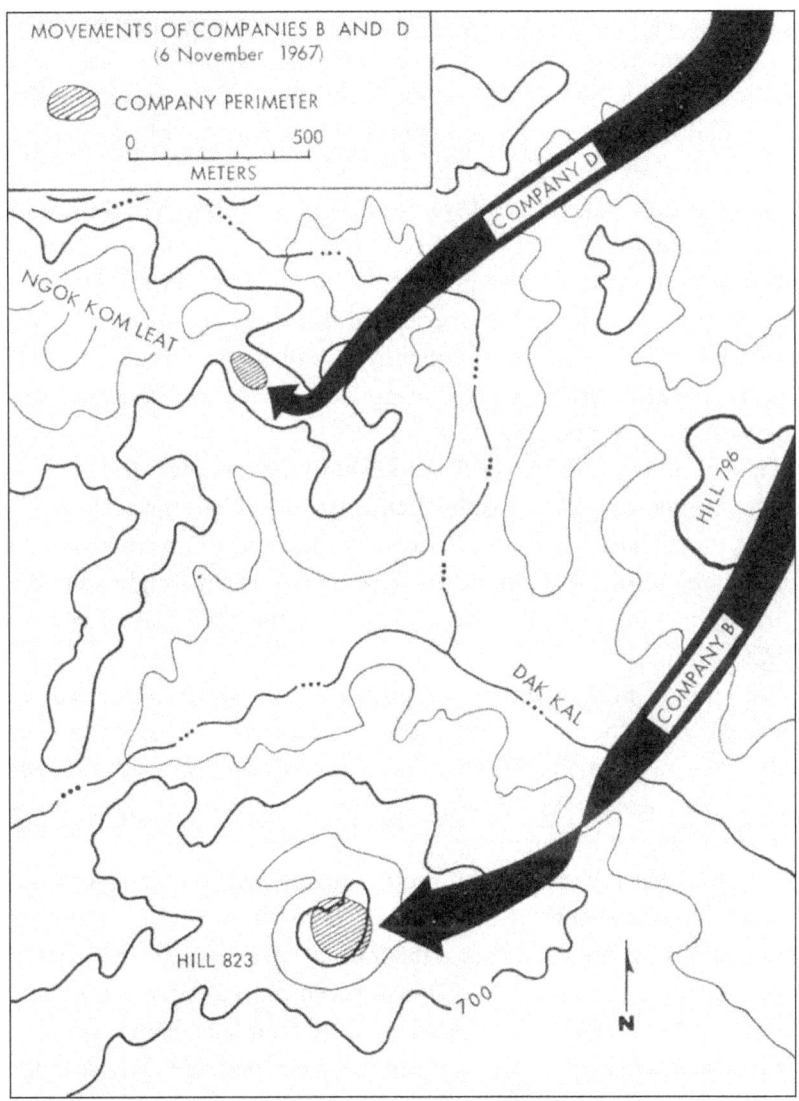

Map 9. Movements of Companies B and D, 6 November 1967

Captain Baird. The platoon of Vietnamese irregulars, because of its central position in the column, at first occupied the forward edge and flanks of the perimeter, but as the tide of combat drew closer they drifted away from Sergeant Ky, back along the trail toward the rear of the perimeter. Baird moved his 1st Platoon up to cover the exposed flanks, while his first sergeant, Sfc. William Collins, began to reorganize the irregulars to cover the rear.

A little later additional assistance to stiffen the Montagnard troops would come from another source: Sergeant Terrazas and his squad from Company A were coming up on the rear of the perimeter. The men had unsuccessfully attempted to follow the trail of their parent unit. Now they homed in on the sounds of combat.

With his rear taken care of and his flanks secured by the 1st Platoon, Baird faced the pressing problem to his front. Although Sergeant Worley's squad successfully pulled back through the 2d and 3d Squads, Burton's entire platoon became locked in a tight fire fight with what the men estimated to be a company of North Vietnamese. Burton's men needed assistance to disengage in order to close the short gap between platoon and company.

Baird called for a tactical air strike, but found all the fighters in his area momentarily unavailable. Helicopter gunships moved in to do what they could to relieve the pressure, and the 105-mm. howitzers of Battery B, 3d Battalion, 319th Artillery, lent their weight from the fire support base six kilometers away. With this help, the 2d Platoon broke away.

Lieutenant Burton with two men and a machine gun covered the withdrawal of the 2d and 3d Squads. After a quarter-hour separation, all the men successfully rejoined Company D and secured the front of the perimeter as the delayed air strike plastered a suspected enemy assembly area atop the hill.

Captain Baird had so organized the position that its long axis was parallel to and slightly left of the trail. Burton's 2d Squad, occupying the right front, was able to cover the trail approach. The 3d Squad faced the left front, and the 1st Squad held down the left flank to the point where it tied in with the 1st Platoon. Seen from above, the company position was oval in shape, astride a knob on the ridge ascending the higher reaches of Ngok Kom Leat. Scrub interspersed with tall trees and clumps of bamboo varied the visibility for each rifleman.

When the 2d Platoon pulled back into the company perimeter, S. Sgts. Michael A. Plank and Edward J. Smith and Spec. 4 Leroy W. Rothwell established themselves in a three-man outpost position fifteen meters to the right front of the 2d Squad sector. From there they angled M16 and M79 fire across the trail and up the hill.

Although the expected assault did not come from up the trail, it did come swiftly.

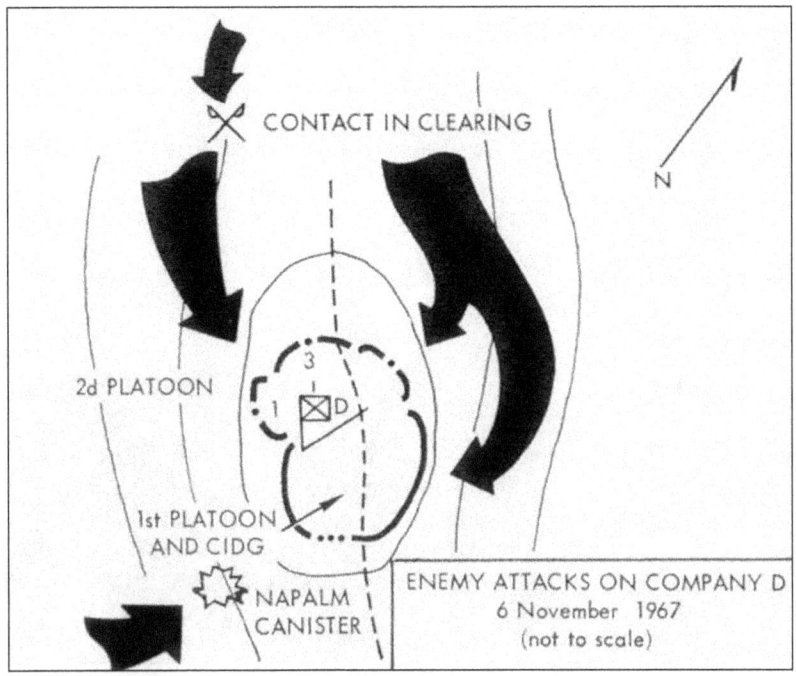

Map 10. Enemy attacks on Company D, 6 November 1967

Suddenly materializing from their jungle concealment, fifteen to twenty of the enemy, their AK47's firing full automatic, rushed at the 2d Squad. Two paratroopers were hit; then the squad leader, Spec. 4 James D. Shafer, took a fatal round. Sergeant Smith rallied the squad and kept the perimeter intact. It was the first bitter taste of things to come.

Minutes later a North Vietnamese force of the same size, struck on the opposite side of the trail, near the left front of the 3d Squad. With flanking fire support from nearby 1st Squad riflemen, the second attack was also repelled. (Map 10)

At the outset of the battle two key figures were wounded. Baird was hit twice in the right wrist and in the upper part of the left arm, injuring the radial nerve but remained in effective command of his company. Capt. Lawrence L. Clewley, forward observer from the 3d Battalion, 3 19th Artillery, was wounded while directing artillery fire. The forward air controller, and, later, Clewley's radio operator, Spec. 4 Ernie L. Fulcher, directed artillery fire for the rest of the day.

At 1400 the sleek F-100's of the 308th Tactical Fighter Squadron hit

Soldiers laying down covering fire with M60

an area just outside the 2d Squad, 1st Platoon, sector with 250-pound bombs, napalm, and 20-mm. cannon shells. Crouching behind a log in front of the squad, Sergeant Smith and his companions in the outpost felt the concussion of the bombs roll over them. It was very close, almost too close for the sergeant. "That second air strike was right in there...," Smith recalled later. "If we'd been on the other side of the log, we wouldn't be here now." A medic who had been crawling toward the outpost was wounded by metal fragments as he vainly shielded the lifeless body of a comrade. Baird and his men knew, however, that the air strikes thus far were instrumental—perhaps decisive in preventing a penetration of the perimeter.

Plank and Rothwell, who had been wounded in the preceding fire fight, moved back from the outpost after the last bomb landed, leaving Smith, who was rapidly expending the last of his ammunition. Sergeant Smith was becoming a favorite target for enemy snipers concealed in tall trees. Spec. 4 Grady L. Madison dashed forward, bringing him badly needed M16 and M79 ammunition. Smith reloaded and fired into some trees to his right. A sniper who had lashed himself to a tree limb tumbled out of his perch; head down, his body swayed grotesquely.

Shortly before 1500, the wounded Rothwell snaked his way back to Smith. Minutes later, with AK47's stuttering, about fifteen North Vietnamese soldiers, bolted from the jungle and charged the 2d Squad. "They came running right at us through the trees and scrub," Rothwell observed later, "...we started knocking them down with our fire, and the rest of the squad really poured it on them." Sergeant Smith added, "Those we didn't hit ran past us to the undergrowth on the right. After they swept past, we heard movement to the right and occasional fire." This wild stampede temporarily ended serious enemy probing in the 2d Platoon area.

At 1510 a reinforced squad of enemy soldiers moved through a stand of bamboo toward the right rear of the Company D perimeter in the 1st Platoon sector. Some Montagnards saw the enemy approaching and Sergeant Ky and several of his men engaged them and drove them off. In repelling this thrust Ky's men were effectively reinforced by Terrazas' squad from Company A. An enemy move against the left rear of the perimeter was halted when a canister of napalm dropped by an F-100 decimated a fifteen-man NVA platoon as it approached the position.

Another hour inched by while the enemy maintained a constant, constricting pressure on the men of Company D. A firing pass by a helicopter gunship wounded one U.S. soldier with inaccurately placed fire when smoke marking the company perimeter failed to rise and clear the high tree canopy. In fact, throughout the afternoon close air support was difficult because marking smoke was frequently not visible to aircraft overhead.

As suddenly as it had begun, the fury of the enemy attack subsided. Although a continuous pattering of sniper fire kicked up spurts of dirt inside the tightly packed position, the perimeter held. A steady crunch of impacting artillery continued to chew up the top of the hill, discouraging any fresh attack in strength from that direction. Over three hours had passed since the fight began and a tenacious adversary still menaced the American position.

Approximately 1,400 meters south of embattled Company D, another scene in the day's drama was well under way. Released from the drudgery of securing one fire support base, the men of Company B at 1320 began to take up the same task again as they occupied

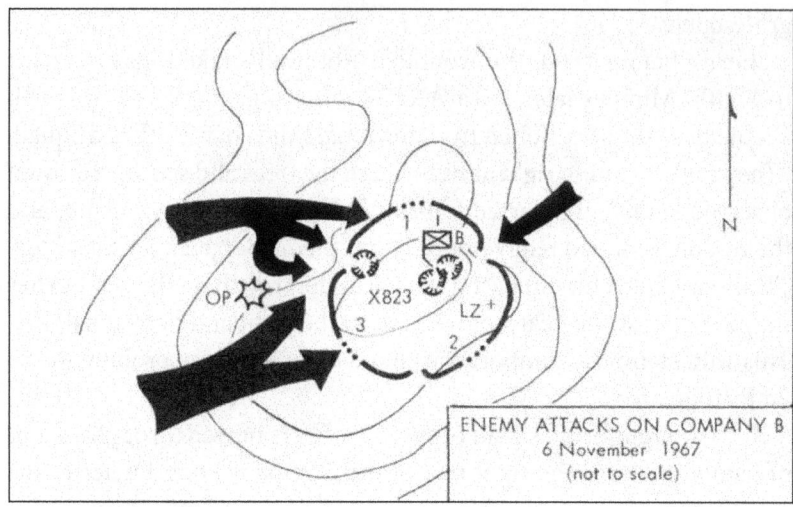

Map 11. Enemy attacks on Company 8, 6 November 1967

forward base, this time by air assault. During the morning five air strikes had failed to clear a landing zone on the selected height, Hill 823, large enough to accommodate even one UH-1D helicopter. When the original assault time of 0900 had long since slipped by, Colonel Johnson requested two or more strikes, and only then were trees and undergrowth sufficiently blasted away to enable one Huey after another, in turn, to hover a few feet off the ground while the occupants jumped into a tangle of shattered bamboo. (See Map 9, page 101)

As the choppers of the 335th Aviation Company disappeared to the east, fresh paratroopers, spared a gruelling cross-country march, made their way up the slope. Atop Hill 823 lead men found several broken rifle stocks and half a dozen North Vietnamese Army rucksacks, evidence that the initial air strikes had caught an enemy force by surprise. This discovery belied an earlier estimate that the hill itself was not occupied by enemy troops.

It was a deserted hilltop now as Capt. George T. Baldridge, the company commander, surveyed his new domain. Hill 823 dominated the ground to nearly all points of the compass. A lush valley separated the hilltop from the ridge where Company D was hanging on. The west and northwest slopes would provide the enemy with comparatively easy approaches to the summit of Hill 823, but the southern slope was too steep for organized assault. Observation was clearest down the southeast slope—fifty meters. Movement on the hill would be hampered severely by broken tree limbs and piles of bamboo.

Captain Baldridge positioned his 1st Platoon where it could defend the northern and northwestern slopes. He disposed his 2d Platoon along the eastern and southern portions of his projected perimeter and in its rear he placed his mortar platoon.

Turning to Lt. Robert H. Darling, Baldridge directed him to move the men of his 3d Platoon up over the crest and a short distance down the hill (about 150 meters from the landing zone), in order to secure the western portion of the perimeter.

Darling was to establish a two-man observation post a hundred meters farther down the hill to provide early warning of an attack along that likely avenue of approach. When his platoon reached its assigned position, Darling sent Pfc. Clarence A. Miller and Spec. 4 Louis C. Miller (they were not related) down the slope to set up the observation post.

Ten minutes later the two Millers were dead.

Darling himself was supervising the distribution of his men along the perimeter when his two-man observation post was struck by a violent fusillade of small arms fire, delivered at close range. With his radio operator and three other hastily designated riflemen, he raced headlong down the slope toward the now silent post. An enemy ambush force of platoon size caught them from their right before they had covered half of the distance. (Map 11)

Captain Baldridge was on the other side of the hill with his 2d Platoon when he heard the distant outbreak of gunfire. His immediate attempt to reach Lieutenant Darling by radio was unsuccessful. Then a voice crackled through company radio receivers—"'November' is hurt bad!" Radio operator Spec. 4 James Ellis was using Darling's code name. It was his last transmission. The lieutenant and all but one man in his impromptu rescue force were dead. Pfc. Robert J. Bickel, although seriously wounded, was able to crawl toward his platoon. His cries for assistance drew not only the attention of his comrades but also that of a small, green-clad enemy soldier who emerged from behind a tree and shot him. His death was avenged when S. Sgt. Alfred McQuirter, covered by two men from his 1st Squad, managed to outflank the enemy rifleman and kill him.

Baldridge later recalled his actions as the attack developed: "I moved forward to the 3d Platoon.... At that point I could hear the gooks laughing and shouting down below. Lieutenant Darling and his men had been hit 30 or 40 meters down from the perimeter." Realizing that his western perimeter was in trouble, Baldridge radioed S. Sgt. Johnnie R. Riley for 60-mm. mortar fire at 100 meters and 81-mm. mortar fire at 250 meters in front of the 3d Platoon. Some mortar men were moved to positions left by members of the 2d Platoon who were being shifted to fill gaps in the 3d Platoon line. Artillery strengthened the developing cordon of fire in front of the beleaguered platoon.

Riley's mortars saved the lives of three men who had belatedly followed Lieutenant Darling's party down the hill. Having made its kill, the NVA ambush party turned its fire on these three soldiers, wounding all of them. Taking cover in a bomb crater, the wounded men exchanged fire with the enemy until two of them ran out of ammunition and the third was about to expend his last magazine. As enemy soldiers closed in, 60-mm. mortar rounds erupted in front of the crater. While their would-be exterminators worried about their own survival, the Americans made it back to the company perimeter and were later evacuated.

Following their initial success, the North Vietnamese pressed the attack up the slope, the NVA tide cresting a few meters in front of the 3d Platoon, near its juncture with the 2d Platoon. Some fifteen determined enemy soldiers made it that far. One of them got near enough to shoot at close range a paratrooper struggling with a jammed M79. The Americans delivered continuous fire on their attackers for twenty minutes before the enemy survivors reeled back down the hill. For some reason, at least thirty North Vietnamese soldiers hiding in heavy, broken bamboo farther down the hill had failed to join in the assault.

During a lull that followed, Sfc. John L. Ponting moved from his position as platoon sergeant, 1st Platoon, to take command of the 3d Platoon. Other men throughout the company also shifted to fill gaps that had opened as a result of the first attack. Reorganization was accomplished swiftly, and fortunately so, for a second attack came at 1515. It was launched from the same direction as the first. Although the attack was quickly repulsed, four more men of the 3d Platoon were wounded.

From a bomb crater at the junction of the 1st and 3d Platoons, men manning a machine gun and a 90-mm. recoilless rifle slammed

173D Airborne Brigade soldiers under fire on Hill 823

flanking fire into the second thrust. Reacting to the effectiveness of these fires, enemy soldiers moved in around the crater and harassed it with grenades during the rest of the day and into the night.

The worst of the fight was over in fifteen minutes, leaving Company B with seven men dead and thirteen wounded. In the next hour all wounded were evacuated by medical helicopters, but the North Vietnamese were still much in evidence in the vicinity of Hill 823, just as they continued to threaten the company over on the slopes of Ngok Kom Leat.

The Company A column, in the meantime, had again moved at a rapid pace that day. Captain Muldoon's men halted only twice during their march. At 1100 the platoon of Montagnards in the lead, supported by fire from the 60-mm. mortars, had an indecisive brush with an eight-to ten-man enemy column. An hour later Nikki, the scout dog, came to alert, but nothing resulted from the search that followed.

At the time when Company D had radioed its request for permission to follow an enemy communications wire, Captain Muldoon was monitoring the net. He was also in radio contact with Sergeant

Terrazas when the latter first came up on the tail of Company D, and he had directed the sergeant to join Company D temporarily.

A few thousand meters to the west, the men of Capt. William J. Connolly's Company C also labored to close on Company D. At 1400 Colonel Johnson directed Connolly to clear the high ground above Captain Baird's embattled perimeter to relieve enemy pressure from the west.

A half hour later Johnson ordered Muldoon to reinforce Company D. At the time the captain was heading toward a selected night defensive position, but he turned and headed west toward the knoll where Baird's company was pinned down. From across the valley Terrazas kept his commander posted on what he could observe of enemy activity between the rear of Company D and the advancing Company A column.

Because the distant sound of automatic weapons, artillery, and air strikes appeared to have a retarding effect on the progress of the leading platoon of irregulars, Muldoon directed 1st Lt. Warren M. Denny to move his point fire team to the head of the column, following it with the balance of his platoon. The Montagnards moved to the side of the tortuous trail to allow the rest of the company passage and re-formed at the rear of the column.

As the company moved across the valley it became increasingly necessary for the four-man point to break trail, frequently by hacking a way through clumps of bamboo. Captain Muldoon ordered his men to drop their rucksacks in order to lighten their loads, planning to return for them once his men had reached Company D and eliminated the enemy threat. Coming up from the valley onto higher ground, the point was in line and the going was somewhat easier.

Two point men, Spec. 4 Herman L. Slaybaugh and Pfc. Dennis T. Ridders, were the first to spot three North Vietnamese soldiers walking in file. Their attempt to stalk the enemy was frustrated when Lieutenant Denny, who had tried without success to reach his point by radio, shouted to them. Startled, the North Vietnamese ran for cover and the point had to open fire, prematurely, hitting only one of the three enemy soldiers.

From up on the ridge Terrazas heard the shots. Taking a compass azimuth toward the sound, he provided his company with an approximate back azimuth to Company D. Shortly thereafter the point discovered the same enemy communications wire that had led their comrades into a fight, and the pace quickened.

It was nearly 1700 as Company A began to close on Company D's perimeter. To the left of the trail, fires smouldered in a small clearing. Fifteen charred enemy bodies scattered around the burned out area gave mute testimony to the effectiveness of the napalm canister dropped two hours earlier.

Captain Muldoon at first established his company in a hasty perimeter defense just below Company D's position, but upon determining the condition of the other company, he deemed it essential that his own men fill gaps in the line. Bringing up his aidmen to minister to the wounded, he co-ordinated with Captain Baird and signalled the rest of his company forward. As the newcomers pulled dead and wounded from the perimeter, occasional automatic weapons fire from North Vietnamese soldiers higher up the hill peppered the area.

Even as the two companies linked, another air strike roared in. As before, the F-100's were accurate, dropping their ordnance close to the wisps of yellow smoke marking the perimeter; yet despite the bombing, every attempt to bring in helicopters to evacuate the wounded encountered heavy fire from automatic weapons.

As dusk drew near and a lull developed in the enemy small arms fire, Muldoon ordered Lieutenant Denny to move his platoon up the hill to find and knock out the enemy gunners. Yet hardly had the first men moved beyond the perimeter when three hidden machine guns rattled a challenge. In the first bursts Denny lost two men killed and three wounded. Not until full darkness descended were the survivors able to crawl back inside the perimeter.

Darkness also enabled helicopters at last to land and pick up the more seriously wounded. Rather than give the enemy further opportunity to pinpoint the defensive position, Captain Muldoon called off the evacuation at 2200.

The enemy continued to fire machine guns at the perimeter. When the American gunners shifted their positions in order to fire more effectively at the enemy's gun flashes, the North Vietnamese switched their own positions. All through the long night enemy hand grenades, rifle grenades, and mortar rounds harassed the two companies, though most of them landed in an open area east of the perimeter. When observers determined that the mortar fire appeared to be coming from the vicinity of a hill 1,200 meters to the southeast, the Americans called down the fire of supporting howitzers. Soon after, the enemy tubes fell silent. Company A's lone 60-mm. mortar did not join in the counter fire lest the muzzle blast afford enemy observers a sound fix on the little perimeter.

Few troopers could drift off to sleep that night of 6 November, for their senses were keyed to the various stimuli of night combat. Spooky, a venerable Air Force AC-47, was on station, dropping flares and raking enemy machine gun positions on a neighboring ridge. Its miniguns—indeed its very presence, droning overhead— gave Spooky a place in every ground soldier's heart. The riflemen also heartened to the cramp of bursting artillery shells as Muldoon and Specialist Fulcher directed the fire of Battery B, 3d Battalion, 319th Artillery, whenever enemy mortars again opened fire, not against Companies A and D but in the direction of Company B on Hill 823.

Company C failed to reach the high ground above Muldoon that day. A 90-minute brush with an enemy blocking force terminated at twilight and Captain Connolly was forced to set up a night defensive position well short of his objective.

While these developments were occurring on the Ngok Kom Leat ridgeline, the North Vietnamese in mid-afternoon of 6 November had stepped up their attack against Company B's perimeter. Colonel Johnson, circling overhead in his helicopter at 1530, watched the company under mortar fire. One round burst near the command post, wounding Captain Baldridge, M. Sgt. Jerry Babb, and six others. Minutes later the battalion commander ordered his pilot to set the chopper down and drop off three of its occupants to provide the company with an interim command group. As Maj. Richard M. Scott, battalion executive officer, Capt. Shirley W. Draper, artillery liaison officer, and Sgt. Maj. Ted G. Arthurs dashed to one of two adjoining bomb craters, Colonel Johnson's helicopter rose in a hail of small arms fire and headed for Ben Het to refuel and evacuate several of the more seriously wounded men of Company B.

Even when the battalion's headquarters company commander, Capt. Ronald R. Leonard, arrived to assume Captain Baldridge's command, Scott and his group remained as a forward battalion command post. Together Scott and Leonard supervised reorganization of Company B's position, including an exchange of positions between

Spooky making a firing pass over Kontum Jungles

the 1st Platoon and the hard-hit ad Platoon in order to strengthen the defense at the vulnerable western avenue of approach. Sniper fire and occasional hand grenades made the reorganization hazardous. Although observers called in mortar and artillery fire close to the perimeter, which suppressed some enemy activity, movement inside the perimeter continued to be risky. While Sergeant Major Arthurs and a recovery detail were trying to retrieve a soldier's body lying a few meters outside the perimeter, an enemy soldier sprang up and threw a grenade. Hitting the dirt to dodge the grenade, the Americans escaped a lethal spray from the soldier's AK47. Sgt. Larry K. Ohda in quick response threw two grenades and killed the enemy soldier.

As dusk approached, men in the crater facing a draw at the juncture of the 1st and 2d Platoons heard sounds of movement in a stand of bamboo in front of them. Cautiously poking his head over the crater rim, one man was startled to see an enemy soldier within five meters of him. Reacting swiftly, he blew the man's head away with a round of M79 canister. This incident presaged a nightlong grenade duel at close range around the perimeter.

Throughout the night, Hill 823 was subjected to a succession of individual and squad-size probes. The 3d Platoon sector on the north, comparatively quiet during daylight hours when the 1st Platoon had defended there, burst into activity after dark. Even though Spooky bathed the hilltop with flare illumination every fifteen minutes, enemy grenades continued to land in front of the platoon. Small teams of North Vietnamese soldiers crept in close enough to cut activating wires for some of the claymore mines that protected Leonard's position. At 0330 from eight to ten North Vietnamese emerged from a gully which led to the point of contact between the 1st and 3d Platoons. Accompanied by a shower of grenades, their sudden assault was supported by RPG2 rocket fire from a nearby hill to the north. The attack nearly succeeded in penetrating the perimeter. It was a short, violent affair; some of the enemy soldiers fell to deadly defensive fire and the rest melted away into the darkness. The Americans lost one man killed, S. Sgt. Joaquine Cabrera, the 1st Platoon sergeant.

Apparently the North Vietnamese had a thorough knowledge of the terrain of Hill 823, but this advantage was somewhat offset by their lack of precise knowledge of the trace of Company B's perimeter. Much of the indirect fire that supported enemy probes went astray, although some rounds landed uncomfortably close to the command group.

The 3d Platoon area continued to be harassed as the night wore on. From foxhole reports Sergeant Panting estimated that up to two squads were moving to the right front. Sounds of movement also came from immediately in front of the platoon. Artillery fire, directed toward the sounds, effectively scattered any would-be attackers. One enemy survivor, after bandaging his partially blown off leg, continued to toss grenades at the Americans until he was killed.

As predawn light began to pierce the darkness, Company B marked its position with smoke, whereupon, like a swarm of angry hornets, helicopter gunships raked enemy positions. They were followed by Air Force F-100's, their explosive loads erupting within 200 meters of the watching paratroopers. It was a welcome sight for the defenders. Napalm plastered an area 300 meters down the ridge, while 20-mm. cannon fire slammed into the enemy threatening the 3d Platoon.

The North Vietnamese nevertheless failed to fade away with the night shadows. At first light, six enemy riflemen with an RPG2 rocket launcher jumped into the bomb crater on the northwest perimeter and attempted to scramble up the inside edge from which they could enfilade two American platoons. When the soldier with the launcher was killed his comrades lost heart and fled. The incident heralded a general exchange of fire along the western perimeter.

When a lull followed, 2d Lt. Hugh M. Proffitt's 2d Platoon began to move over through the 1st Platoon, west, along the southern slope of the finger.

Its mission was to pick up enemy weapons and make a body count. When a burst of small arms fire greeted the platoon, Sergeant Riley's mortars belched fifteen rounds to help the paratroopers silence the enemy riflemen. Resuming the sweep, Proffitt's platoon continued to move along the southern slope then north over the top of the finger. A hundred meters out they discovered foxholes and bunkers with overhead cover. Rucksacks and intrenching tools littered the site. Here was one reason for the enemy's tenacity—his unwillingness to abandon a carefully prepared position. Climbing up a rope ladder leading into the upper reaches of a tall tree, one man gained a clear view of the American fire support base, seven kilometers away.

Closer in, enemy bodies marked the high tide of the enemy's effort. Some of the still-living human debris that the tide had deposited remained along the west slope. It took several forays to ferret out wounded enemy soldiers who continued to fight. With one group of volunteer searchers went the scout dog and his handler. Despite a shower of white phosphorus hand grenades a North Vietnamese officer, still full of fight, lurched from a cave but was gunned down as he made his break.

Although occasional harassing fire reminded Company B's men that remnants of the North Vietnamese force remained around Hill 823, the fight for that promontory was at an end. The Americans had prevailed.

The enemy on Ngok Kom Leat had in the meantime disappeared with the coming of daylight on 7 November. Captain Muldoon's men spent most of the day searching the area, bringing in supplies, and moving wounded comrades to waiting helicopters. Muldoon's two companies linked up with Company C that morning as it came up from the west.

Although Colonel Johnson had intended to consolidate all companies of his battalion during the day on the new, hard-won fire support base, the crash of a resupply helicopter as it was leaving Ngok Kom Leat and the requirement to secure its radios, machine guns, and other equipment forced him to delay the move. But now reinforcements for Company B were available from another source. The commander of the 173d Airborne Brigade, newly arrived in Dak To, made another company available. At midday helicopters brought Company C, 1st Battalion, 503d Infantry, to Hill 823.

The next day, 8 November, Colonel Johnson at last got his entire 4th Battalion, 503d Infantry, together again on the hill. Although he intended pursuing the enemy toward the west, his superiors deemed it time the battalion had a short rest. That afternoon and the following day the 1st Battalion, 503d Infantry, phased in to replace Johnson's men.

The fights on the Ngok Kom Leat and Hill 823 were but opening rounds in a battle that was to continue in the vicinity of Dak To for two and a half weeks, but in those rounds the 4th Battalion, 503d Infantry, had driven at least a portion of the North Vietnamese 66th Regiment back toward the Cambodian border and materially lessened the threat to Dak To. The cost to the Americans was 15 men killed and 48 wounded. The North Vietnamese had lost at least 117 men killed, 1 prisoner, 44 individual weapons (mainly AK47's), 7 machine guns, and 5 RPG2 rocket launchers.

6. Battle of Lang Vei
5 May 1968

BY JOHN A. CASH

Deep in the reinforced concrete bunker that served as a tactical operations center, Capt. Frank C. Willoughby, a young Green Beret detachment commander, studied the acetate-covered operations map on the wall before him while he held a telephone to his ear. Power generators and radio static buzzed in the background. In the dim light his wristwatch glowed 1932. He knew that it was now dark in the camp above him, but here in the bunker it was always night. He put down the telephone; two of his defensive positions had just reported hearing noises that sounded like engines idling, and he was now convinced that an enemy attack was not far off. It was 6 February 1968, only a few days since the Free World forces had felt the fury of the unexpected Tet (lunar new year) offensive the entire length of South Vietnam. All the signs of another enemy attack were there. In the middle of the morning a mortar barrage had slammed into his camp without warning, wounding eight Vietnamese soldiers. In the early evening, fifty rounds of enemy 152-mm. artillery fire from across the Laotian border had wounded two more soldiers and heavily damaged two bunkers. Since then he had received frequent reports of strange noises and trip flare booby traps going off.

But exactly where and when would the enemy hit?

As a precaution, Willoughby radioed an alert to the Khe Sanh Marine Base, a few kilometers away to the northeast. Whatever the enemy planned, he expected that the big guns at Khe Sanh would make it costly.

Just after midnight, shrouded by the blackness, five Soviet built PT76 medium tanks crept steadily north up a narrow trail from the shell-scarred village of Lang Troai, less than a kilometre south of Willoughby's camp. Behind them, wearing green uniforms and steel helmets, their weapons at the ready, two platoons of heavily armed North Vietnamese infantrymen followed in the dust and exhaust

117

raised by the tanks.

As the first two tanks, their commanders perched in the cupolas, reached the barbed-wire barrier that outlined the camp, a trip flare ignited, bathing the green metal tanks and dust-covered soldiers in an eerie flickering light. For a second both the camp's defenders and the enemy force were transfixed, staring at each other, then both sides began firing furiously.

The battle for Lang Vei had begun.

Tucked away in the northwest corner of Quang Tri Province, in densely wooded, rugged terrain of the I Corps tactical zone, Lang Vei seemed a likely place for a Free World outpost. It was thirty-five kilometers south of the Demilitarized Zone and one and a half kilometers east of the Xe Pone River, the Laotian border. To the northeast, eight kilometers away, was the Marine combat base at Khe Sanh. The Lang Vei Special Forces Camp was south of Lang Vei Village, built along a stretch of Highway 9, a major east-west, all-weather road. (See Map 1 on page 8)

Under the control of the 5th Special Forces Group, the Lang Vei Camp had been conceived as a base from which to administer the local Civilian Irregular Defense Group (CIDG) program to train and equip locally recruited Vietnamese. These irregulars would operate in the remote, sparsely populated, contested areas where they could be more effectively used than Vietnamese Army and other Free World forces. By late 1967, working jointly with Vietnamese Special Forces teams, twelve-man American Special Forces A detachments were operating sixty-four CIDG camps throughout Vietnam, from Lang Vei in the north to Phu Quoc Island, some sixty kilometers off the southern coast in the Gulf of Siam.

Willoughby's Detachment A-101 at Lang Vei was one of nine CIDG operational camps active in the I Corps tactical zone. From Da Nang, over 150 kilometers south, Company C, 5th Special Forces, the next higher headquarters, had assigned Willoughby a tactical area of responsibility of 220 square kilometers. Within this zone Willoughby's detachment, working jointly with a fourteen-man Vietnamese Special Forces contingent and six interpreters, was responsible for border surveillance, interdiction of enemy infiltration routes, and assistance in pacification—the Revolutionary Development Program. To accomplish these tasks, Willoughby had a camp strike force of one

Montagnard and four Vietnamese rifle companies and three combat reconnaissance platoons. These units ranged the entire tactical area, from time to time engaging in minor skirmishes with the enemy.

Detachment A-101 had originally been established in July 1962 at Khe Sanh. The camp had remained operational until December 1966, when it was moved west to a site near the village of Lang Vei so that marines could occupy Khe Sanh as part of an American troop build-up in the northern provinces. The first camp established at Lang Vei proved to be temporary. A ground force of North Vietnamese regulars, aided by a well-organized group that infiltrated the CIDG troops within the camp itself, penetrated the camp on 4 May 1967. Both the detachment commander and his executive officer were killed. Although the enemy failed to seize the post, damage was extensive. Because major reconstruction would have been required and since the site itself, as the attack revealed, lacked good observation and fields of fire beyond the barbed-wire perimeter, the commander of the Special Forces Group decided to relocate the base at a more suitable place about 1,000 meters to the west. The new camp on Highway 9 near Lang Vei was completed in late September 1967.

While Captain Willoughby's men worked to strengthen the new camp's defenses throughout the fall, his patrols made relatively few contacts with the enemy. In December 1967, however, reliable sources reported large enemy concentrations in Laos, only a few kilometers away, and patrols based on Lang Vei made more frequent contacts with the enemy. By mid-January intelligence agents warned that enemy battalions were infiltrating across the Xe Pone River, their destination Khe Sanh. At the same time, artillery and mortar fire began to harass the Lang Vei Camp at least two or three times a week and small enemy patrols sometimes probed the perimeter.

On 21 January 1968, after a brief fight, the village of Khe Sanh fell into North Vietnamese hands, and the next day scores of civilian refugees began to descend on the CIDG camp and the nearby village of Lang Veil A few days later, on the 24th, survivors of the 33d Royal Laotian Battalion and their dependents, 2,700 in all, streamed into Willoughby's camp from the west, with tales that an enemy tank-infantry force had overrun their camp.

With an estimated 8,000 non-combatants within a thousand meters of his camp, all expecting some aid from him, Willoughby radioed

Da Nang for assistance. The following day help arrived in the form of a six-man Special Forces augmentation team with medical supplies and food. Willoughby assigned the new team to the Laotians, whom he provided with ammunition and with barrier materials and tools to refortify the old Lang Vei Camp, where they would remain until he received further instructions from Da Nang. While the adviser team inoculated the Laotians against cholera, Willoughby's men distributed rice, powdered milk, and other essential food supplies, a task that was to continue indefinitely. The new refugees crowded into Lang Vei Village and the small settlements around it.

Since the Laotians' base camp was only fifteen kilometers away on Highway 9 in Laos, the news of the tank attack caused Willoughby some concern. It shed light on an earlier report from a forward air controller who had sighted five enemy tanks moving away from the scene of the battle and had called in an air strike which destroyed one. Although Willoughby assumed that the Marine combat base at Khe Sanh was the enemy's primary objective, he realized that any sensible enemy force would have to do something about his camp.

His fears were confirmed when a North Vietnamese deserter turned up at Lang Vei on 30 January and revealed after questioning that he had been a member of a reconnaissance team from a North Vietnamese battalion bivouacked just across the river in Laos. The team had reconnoitred Lang Vei's defenses the night of the 28th, he said, specifically to pinpoint heavy and automatic weapons positions. An attack had been planned and cancelled twice for reasons unknown to the Vietnamese captive. There were tracked vehicles positioned near his battalion.

Willoughby had done what he could to safeguard his small post by stepping up his nightly ambushes and daylight patrols. His resources were meager, however, for he had been able to recruit only 65 percent of the strength authorized for his three companies and three platoons. Earlier in January Company C had reinforced him with a 161-man mobile strike force company of Hre tribesmen along with six Green Beret advisers. By the middle of the month Willoughby had disposed a platoon of this crack outfit at an early warning outpost, 800 meters west of the camp, in fortified bunkers with overhead cover, surrounded by barbed wire and claymore mines. The Hre Montagnards patrolled during the day and occupied ambush positions in the vicinity of the camp at night. The other two of the company's three platoons operated from Lang Vei Camp itself.

Willoughby's camp was well designed for defense and he had decided to keep non combatants out of it. Resembling a dog bone when viewed from above, the installation had been constructed under the "fighting camp" concept. (Map 12 overleaf) A careful analysis had been made of probable enemy courses of action and of how best to use the terrain and employ troops and firepower. As in the case of the previous Lang Vei Camp, the base would be defended by one-third of its strength while the other two-thirds operated in the tactical area of responsibility. Although in late January some individual positions and bunkers were still being constructed, or repaired because of the damage inflicted by enemy artillery and mortar fire, the entire camp was ringed by a strong three-layer barbed-wire barrier fifty meters wide, laced with claymore mines emplaced at maximum effective small arms range. All completed bunkers and individual positions were heavily sandbagged on all sides and overhead. All fighting positions had excellent fields of fire, so situated that enemy troops would find it costly to attack up the hillside.

Within the defenses, Willoughby had placed his companies and platoons in mutually supporting positions, each with American advisers from the detachment. Each company and platoon position within the perimeter was further enclosed with barbed wire and ringed by claymore mines and trip flares.

On the northeastern flank he placed his Company 101 of eighty-two Bru tribesmen. South of it he placed his Company 104, whose strength was, as in other units, actually little more than that of a reinforced rifle platoon. At the opposite end of the compound, 450 meters to the west, he located his Company 102, forty-two men, while just to the south and contiguous to the position he placed the forty-three men of Company 103. Since Willoughby considered Company 101 his weakest unit because of its leadership, he put his 3d Combat Reconnaissance Platoon behind it as a backup force, placing the 1st and 2d Reconnaissance Platoons on the northern and southern perimeter, respectively, 200 meters apart.

In terms of firepower, Willoughby was well prepared. For heavy indirect fire support for the entire base, he had two 4.2-inch mortars with over 800 high-explosive and illumination rounds. Each company

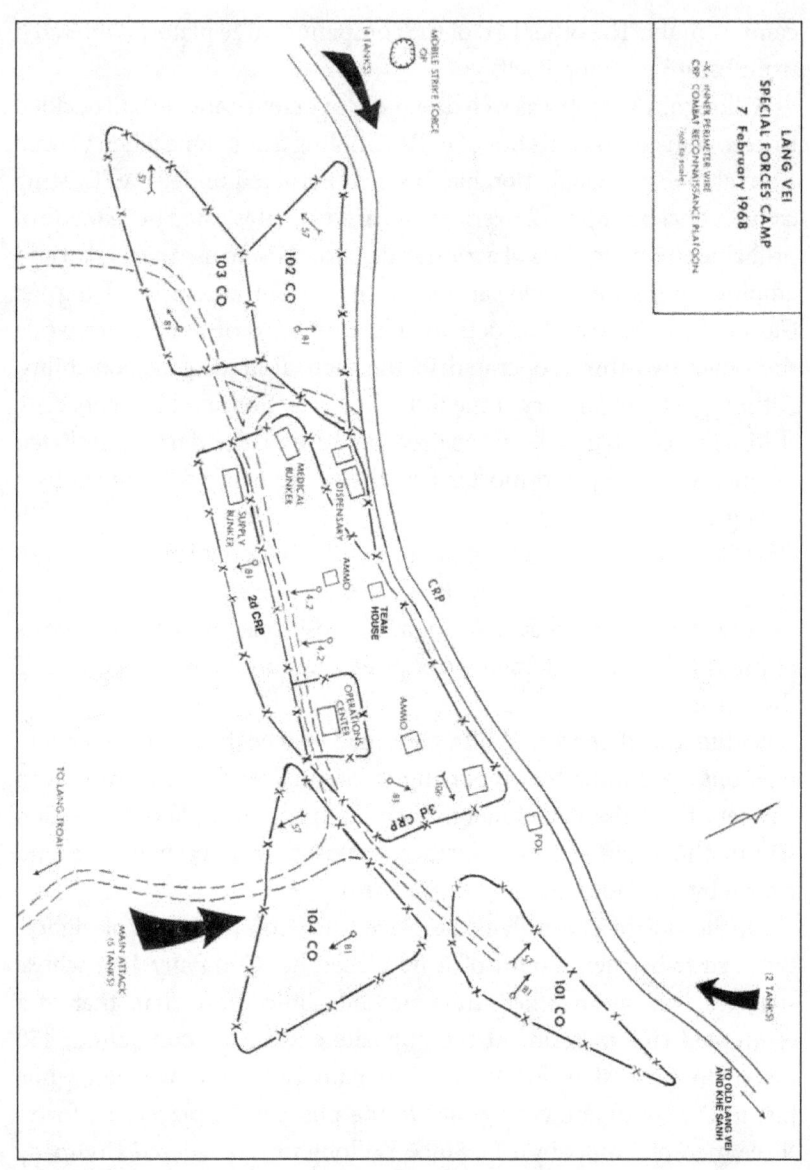

Map 12. Lang Vei Special Forces Camp, 7 February 1968

and platoon area had one 81-mm. mortar for which 2,000 assorted rounds of ammunition were available. Nineteen 60-mm. mortars were positioned strategically throughout the camp, with nearly 3,000 high-explosive rounds on hand.

The mainstay of Willoughby's antitank defense were two 106-mm. recoilless rifles. One was in the 2d Combat Reconnaissance Platoon sector to cover the southern road into the camp from Lang Troai Village. The other was in the ad Reconnaissance Platoon sector where it could place flanking fire on any vehicles moving along Highway 9. Each weapon had more than twenty high-explosive rounds. Supplementing them were four 57-mm. recoilless rifles, one for each company area for which he had stockpiled over 3,000 rounds, 2,800 of them deadly canister projectiles. Finally, for close-in antitank defense, a hundred M72's—light assault weapons—(LAW'S) were strategically placed throughout the camp. (The LAW is a one-shot, disposable launcher-container, loaded with a shaped charge round and fired from the shoulder.)

Detachment A-101 had an impressive number of crew-served automatic weapons. For general support of the post, one .50-caliber machine gun was set on top of the detachment's living quarters, the "team house," just behind the 1st Reconnaissance Platoon, where it covered the northern approaches to the camp. In the 2d Reconnaissance Platoon area another .50-caliber machine gun covered the southern approaches and could reinforce the 106-mm. recoilless rifle fire in that direction, especially along the Lang Troai Village road. For the two machine guns there were over 17,000 rounds available.

The CIDG companies and platoons were armed with forty-seven .30-caliber machine guns and more than 275,000 rounds of ball ammunition; thirty-nine Browning automatic rifles (BAR'S) with close to 200,000 rounds; and two M60 machine guns with 5,000 rounds.

Individually, CIDG troops carried M1 and M2 carbines for which almost 250,000 rounds were on hand—enough for three basic loads per man, with a resupply stockpiled at company level. Also available were almost 1,000 fragmentation grenades, 390 claymore mines, and 250 12-gauge shotgun rounds for the few shotguns on hand.

For artillery support, Willoughby could call on sixteen 175-mm. guns, sixteen 155-mm. guns, and eighteen 105-mm. howitzers from Khe Sanh and other locations within range. Well before the end of

4.2-Inch mortar

January, a variety of concentrations had been registered in, with particular emphasis on likely avenues of approach and suspected enemy staging areas.

Ready for close-in support, if needed, were Marine all-weather (radar-controlled) fighter aircraft. U.S. Air Force planes might be called on as well, among them the deadly Spooky with its illuminating flares and rapid-fire miniguns.

If necessary Willoughby could request at least two rifle companies from the 26th Marine Regiment, based at Khe Sanh. Provided that the tactical situation at Khe Sanh allowed it, these companies were prepared to move on short notice by foot or helicopter to previously selected landing zones as part of an already rehearsed reaction plan. Also, Da Nang Company C, 5th Special Forces headquarters stood ready to send in another mobile strike force company if the need arose.

These were the resources of the Lang Vei Special Forces Camp when the enemy's Tet offensive struck it during the early morning hours of 7 February 1968.

The five-tank contingent that advanced on Willoughby's fortress formed the main effort of a sizable attacking force. Supported by at least four 152-mm. artillery pieces and four 82-mm. mortars, two other columns were also advancing on the camp: four tanks and two North Vietnamese infantry platoons surged toward Companies 102 and 103, while two tanks advanced on Company 101 from the north.

Perhaps the first American to see the enemy was Willoughby's 24-year-old assistant medical specialist, Sgt. Nickolas Fragos.

Manning an observation post in a tower above the tactical operations center when the tanks first approached the wire along the Lang Troai road, Fragos could hardly believe his eyes. In the flickering flare light he saw two North Vietnamese soldiers kneeling calmly in front of the lead tank, attempting to breach the barbed-wire barrier in front of Company 104. "Why don't they let the tank treads crush the wire?" wondered Fragos dazedly. Before his eyes the two enemy soldiers slumped over dead, cut down by the Company 104 defenders.

Fragos radioed Willoughby. "We have tanks in our wire!"

That done, he rushed down into the operations center and described what he had seen to Captain Willoughby. Lt. Col. Daniel F. Schungel, the Company C commander from Da Nang, listened incredulously. He was in the camp by chance, having arrived early in the afternoon of the previous day on a visit that was primarily a gesture of diplomacy toward the Laotian battalion commander, who was also a lieutenant colonel. Colonel Schungel, accompanied by Willoughby and the Vietnamese operations officer of the camp, had inspected the defenses the preceding day and believed at the time that the camp was well prepared. Now he raced up the concrete steps to see the tanks for himself. Willoughby and Fragos followed. They stared in amazement at an enemy tank, its main gun blasting away at Company 104 bunkers, then rushed back down into the operations center.

Schungel told Willoughby to concentrate all available artillery and air support on the massed force just in front of Company 104. He also told him to request a flagship and to ask for everything through parallel channels, the marines at Khe Sanh and Company C. Colonel Schungel then hurried back upstairs to join the fight and to organize "tank-killer" teams.

The enemy seemed everywhere. Small arms and automatic weapons fire rattled from all sides. Plodding inexorably forward, the enemy tanks swept the camp with machine gun fire and high-explosive cannon rounds. Behind them the North Vietnamese infantrymen crept slowly, deploying and firing their AK47 automatic rifles into positions marked for them by tracer machine gun fire and searchlight beams from the tanks.

Willoughby's men returned fire furiously. Moments after the attack began, Sfc. James W. Holt, the team's senior medic, was at his duty post in the 2d Reconnaissance Platoon area. He trained the 106-mm. recoilless rifle on the lead tanks and in the glare of an 81-mm. illuminating round scored direct hits on both of them at less than 350 meters. As the tanks began to burn, enemy crewmen, including three women armed with M16 rifles, climbed from escape hatches and raced for cover. Reloading, Holt blasted away at the enemy with three "Beehive" rounds, and Colonel Schungel and CIDG riflemen helped to pick the enemy off with hand grenades, LAW's, and rifles.

Still other enemy troops pressed forward. A third tank appeared, swung around the two flaming hulks, and, its coaxial tracer rounds beating a deadly pattern, crashed through the barbed wire and into the Company 104 sector.

A few meters behind Sergeant Holt, S. Sgt. Peter Tirach, the detachment intelligence sergeant, was at one of the 4.2-inch mortar pits. Tirach and two junior radio operators, Spec. 4 Franklin H. Dooms and S. Sgt. Dennis L. Thompson, and Sfc. Earl F. Burke, a platoon leader with the mobile strike force company, had been firing illumination and high-explosive rounds, the latter as close as possible behind the enemy tanks, in the hope of stopping the accompanying infantry. Seeing that Holt was alone at the 106 and figuring that there were more than enough men to do the job at the mortar position, Sergeant Tirach scrambled to Holt's side and helped him load another round into the weapon. It was the last high-explosive round at the

Light assault weapon carried on a soldier's back

position. Traversing slowly, Holt aimed at the third tank and fired, scoring a direct hit and immobilizing it, but not before the tank had destroyed at least three bunkers in the Company 104 area.

Since there was no more high-explosive ammunition, Tirach returned to the 4.2-inch mortar pit while Holt ran toward the team house a hundred meters to the north. Holt was never seen alive again.

No sooner had both sergeants left than another enemy PT76 churned up the Lang Troai road at top speed and into the breach in the wire. Grinding to a halt, the tank fired point-blank at the 106-mm.

recoilless rifle, destroying it. Soon joined by another tank, the PT76 rumbled forward into the Company 104 area.

Down in the operations center, Willoughby had been trying to get artillery fire support. Because Khe Sanh itself was under artillery attack and U.S. Marine headquarters there wanted more information as to the size of the enemy force attacking Lang Vei, there was a delay. The fight was fifteen minutes old before the first artillery rounds smashed just outside the camp perimeter. With various team members above him observing and adjusting the bright quick flashes, Willoughby relayed target corrections to the marines, who fired volley after volley of high-explosive and illumination rounds in response. Since Willoughby considered the enemy thrust against Company 104 to be the enemy's main effort, he concentrated the artillery firepower there in the early stage of the battle.

By 0100, ten minutes after the artillery had begun firing, a U.S. Air Force forward air controller arrived, along with a flareship and a Spooky gunship. Circling the camp, the controller radioed to Willoughby that fighter aircraft were on the way. They arrived moments later. At Willoughby's request, the controller directed air strikes along the ravine north of the camp, on the Lang Troai road just south of it, and to the west of the mobile strike force early warning outpost.

Despite the air strikes, continuing artillery support, and courageous efforts by the men on the ground, the situation steadily worsened for Lang Vei's defenders. Enemy soldiers succeeded in exploiting the tank penetration into the Company 104 area, forcing its defenders to pull back into the 2d and 3d Platoon position behind them, which in turn exposed the southern flank of Company 101.

Seizing this advantage, the North Vietnamese troops poured a murderous fire into Company 101 from their newly captured Company 104 positions. Two more tanks soon added to the fire and an infantry company attacked Company 101 from the north. Automatic weapons flashed and mortar shells threw up geysers of earth.

Just as the attacking troops reached the barbed-wire perimeter, Willoughby called for the nearest artillery concentration. The first volley landed in the center of the camp, but he adjusted it quickly so that the fire fell into the enemy's ranks, stopping the assault for the moment. The enemy fire from the Company 104 area, along with the shock effect of the two tanks, proved, however, too much for the CIDG defenders, who retreated to the 3d Platoon positions behind them. Thus by 0115 the entire eastern end of the camp was in enemy hands.

At the other end of the camp the situation was just as desperate. Three enemy tanks had smashed through the barbed-wire barrier facing Companies 102 and 103. At point-blank range the tanks began destroying bunkers, while behind them two platoons of North Vietnamese exploited the havoc the tanks had wrought. The heavy crackle of several automatic weapons sounded everywhere. Although the CIDG defenders fought courageously, they were no match for the determined enemy with his armored support. In short order both companies were overrun, exposing the western end of the camp. Survivors, still fighting, withdrew, some heading toward the reconnaissance platoon positions while others moved toward Highway 9, hoping to make it to Khe Sanh, to the east.

Nor was the situation any better at the mobile strike force observation post, 800 meters west of the camp. Sfc. Charles W. Lindewald, an adviser with the platoon-size force, had radioed Willoughby that he was being attacked by at least a company and possibly two tanks just as the enemy force had smashed into Company 104. Believing the outpost in danger of encirclement, Lindewald called for artillery fire. A few moments later a machine gun bullet hit him in the stomach. While Sfc. Kenneth Hanna, Willoughby's heavy weapons sergeant, administered first aid, Lindewald directed artillery fire on the enemy force that was snaking toward his position. Lindewald died as North Vietnamese soldiers seized the hill. Hanna was captured by the soldiers and never seen again.

Inside the Lang Vei Camp, Colonel Schungel's hastily organized tank-killer teams were ready by the time Holt had destroyed his second tank. After leaving the operations center, Schungel had collected 1st Lt. Paul R. Longgrear, who commanded the mobile strike company and had been busy at the Number 2 81-mm. mortar pit; First Lieutenant Quy, the Vietnamese operations officer; and 1st Lt. Miles R. Wilkins, Willoughby's executive officer, who had been at the second 4.2-inch mortar position in the 2d Combat Reconnaissance Platoon sector. A junior radio operator, Spec. 5 William G. McMurray, and Sergeant Fragos, along with a few Civilian Irregular troops, joined the group. Arming themselves with LAW's, they fanned out as two-man teams in search of targets.

Schungel had even snatched up a few LAW's and fired at the first two tanks before Halt had, but with little effect. Under the intermittent glare of green tracer bullets fired from an enemy 12.7mm. machine gun somewhere to the north, Schungel and Fragos lay prone near the operations center, firing until their small supply of LAW's was exhausted, but without apparent effect on the enemy tanks. Schungel, concerned about the two tanks that now roamed the Company 104 area at will, yelled to Fragos to get more LAW's.

Crawling to the nearest 4.2-inch mortar pit, Fragos snatched four more and dragged them by their carrying straps back to Schungel's position. He gave two to the officer and kept the other two for himself. Moving a few meters away from Colonel Schungel to avoid endangering him with the backblast, Fragos jerked one of the weapons to his shoulder, squinted through the sight, and fired at the nearest of two tanks, perhaps seventy-five meters away. With a dull metallic click the weapon misfired. Casting the dud aside, Fragos snatched the other LAW and fired. With a muffled explosion, the projectile buried itself in the earth ahead of the tank's front tracks. Too short! Fragos scurried back to Colonel Schungel's position just as a burst of machine gun tracers blasted the spot where he had been.

Fragos found Schungel trying to remove the safety from a LAW. He tried it himself but to no avail. While other tank-killer teams fired at least five missiles at the still-advancing tanks but failed to stop them, Fragos rushed down into the operations center in search of a sharp instrument to use on the jammed safety.

Inside the center, Fragos picked his way among the wounded— six Americans and a number of South Vietnamese who lay sprawled about on the floor. Across the crowded room, he called to Willoughby, who was occupied at his radio that green tracers from heavy machine guns were coming from the north.

Sizing up the probable machine gun position from what Fragos told him, Willoughby immediately radioed the marines' supporting artillery for a variable time mission from all available guns just north of the Company 104 area, outside the wire. In seconds he received an "on the way" from the marines.

Unable to locate a suitable tool with which to remove his LAW's safety clip, Fragos left the weapon in the operations center and rejoined the battle above. He was just in time to see Colonel Schungel, on one knee, calmly taking aim and then firing a missile at the still-advancing lead tank. In a shower of bright orange sparks, the rocket smashed broadside against the tank. Yet the tank, apparently undamaged, continued to dash about amidst the bunkers of Company 104.

Frustrated, Schungel grabbed another LAW, and with Fragos raced after the tank to get a closer shot. Spec. 4 James L. Moreland, a medic with the mobile strike force who had observed the action from the team house, joined them. When he thought he was close enough, Schungel fired his remaining weapon. Misfire! Desperately, amidst a hail of enemy small arms and machine gun fire, the three Americans fired their M16's at the tank's apertures and tossed grenades at its treads, but to no avail. Seemingly contemptuous of this minor harassment, the enemy tank continued to blast away at bunkers and fighting positions. Unless the tank could be stopped, it would soon leave the Company 104 positions and enter the camp's inner perimeter. Amidst crackling gunfire and an almost continuous roar of explosions, a voice yelled for plastic explosive. Perhaps someone could get close enough to the tank to immobilize it with a well-placed charge. Specialist Moreland and Sergeant Fragos ran for the ammunition bunker on the western side of the 2d Combat Reconnaissance Platoon area where an ample supply of explosives was stored, but as they passed the 4.2-inch mortar pit, an enemy artillery round landed in a fuel dump next to the ammunition bunker. The dump exploded with a roaring flame, belching thick, boiling, black smoke skyward. The path to the ammunition now blocked, Moreland and Fragos turned back toward the center, picking up two LAW's on the way.

The time was now approximately 0430.

The crew of the second tank, perhaps encouraged by the display of invulnerability exhibited by the lead tank, had meanwhile edged their tank closer to the rear limits of the Company 104 area; now it stopped less than 100 meters from the operations center. With North Vietnamese infantrymen crouched behind it, and its turret rotating slowly from side to side, the tank fired its machine gun in short staccato bursts, sweeping the camp.

Through a black billow of smoke that rolled across the camp, Sergeant Tirach, still at the first 4.2-inch mortar pit, spotted the tank, and, realizing that from his position he had a clear shot, steadied himself in a semi-kneeling posture at the edge of the pit parapet,

A destroyed PT76 tank.

aimed a LAW, and squeezed the trigger. Another misfire.

The Lang Vei defenders' heroic efforts to blunt the tank attack had thus far been futile. Although the tanks had not yet entered the inner perimeter, it was in grave danger.

From atop the team house, Sergeant Tiep, one of the detachment's Vietnamese interpreters, yelled that another tank was heading toward him. Peering into the darkness from his position at the second 4.2-inch mortar pit, Lieutenant Wilkins, alerted by Tiep's warning, saw a PT76 tank hurrying westward along Highway 9. It was one of the tanks that had figured in the attack against Company 101. Since the 106-mm. recoilless rifle in the 3d Combat Reconnaissance Platoon area had already been destroyed by enemy fire, Wilkins decided to attack the tank himself. With two LAW's he rushed forward to a better firing position, arriving just as the tank ground to a halt on the road, abreast of the team house. As Wilkins raised one of his weapons to fire it a Vietnamese appeared from nowhere pointed excitedly at the tank, and shouted, "CIDG, CIDG!" Thinking for an instant that some of the detachment's defenders had captured the tank, the lieutenant lowered his weapon. His hopes fell, however, when the vehicle started with a jerk and continued on its way. Wilkins suddenly realized that the Civilian Irregular Defense Group men had no tank training and would hardly be operating a tank. He fired, scoring a hit on the front end. Apparently undamaged, the tank halted again, while its turret turned in search of its tormentors. When the tank resumed its run, Wilkins tried again, but this time his weapon misfired.

Resupplied with an armful of LAW's that Sergeant Burke rushed to him from the team house, Wilkins followed the tank toward Company 102, firing rockets as he moved and scoring hits that did not stop the tank. Sergeant Thompson fired his M79 grenade launcher at the tank's treads. Sergeant Tirach tossed grenades at its underside. Other men climbed on top of the tank and attempted to force grenades into its hatches. But the tank continued onward, immune to the weapons of the Lang Vei defenders.

While Captain Willoughby's force was under heavy siege, the Laotian survivors and their six American advisers at the old camp site were faring much better. Either the enemy was unaware that the old camp, which lay about a kilometre east of the new camp, was occupied or they did not think a diversionary attack against it was worth the effort. Except for a U.S. Air Force 250-pound bomb and a few mortar rounds, the old camp had received no heavy fire. Frustrated, anxious to help their beleaguered comrades, the Americans there monitored the battle by radio, attempting to determine the course of the fighting. By 0130 Sgt. Richard H. Allen, an assistant medical specialist, had persuaded the Laotian battalion commander to fire 81-mm. illumination rounds over the fighting. A few moments later, Spec. 4 Joel Johnson, another assistant medical specialist, saw the two enemy tanks and infantrymen blasting away at Company 101 from the north. Determined not to see the camp fall, Specialist Johnson asked Sfc. Eugene Ashley, an intelligence non-commissioned officer and their leader, for fifty Laotian soldiers and a 3.5-inch rocket launcher. He wanted to attack the tanks from behind. Ashley, agreeing with the plan, took him to the Laotian battalion commander, who decided against sending troops before daylight.

It was about 0245 when one of the tanks in the Lang Vei Camp that had figured in the attack against Company 103 rolled toward the operations center. Enemy armor had finally broken through the inner perimeter.

An Engineer officer from Da Nang headquarters, 1st Lt. Thomas E. Todd, saw the tank as it passed his vantage point, the emergency medical bunker. He had been at the camp since the afternoon of the 5th, his mission to supervise the repair of shell-damaged defenses. In an effort to join in the fighting, he had been searching for hand grenades.

The tank stopped, swung its turret around, and blasted away point-blank at the front entrance of the medical bunker. Shell fragments whined through the air. Another tank approached, followed by about fifty enemy soldiers. It too stopped, fired at the rear entrance, and then lumbered on. Luckily, Todd suffered only a minor wound. Since it appeared to him that the enemy had control of the entire camp, he decided to remain hidden in the bunker until daylight.

Another enemy tank from Company 104's area had meanwhile penetrated the inner perimeter wire near the Number 2 81-mm. mortar, a stone's throw from the operations center. Destroying the mortar position, the tank headed straight for the operations center, followed by North Vietnamese infantrymen. Willoughby's command bunker was now threatened from two directions.

For all the one-sidedness of the battle, Lang Vei's defenders still had plenty of fight in them. When the tanks approached the operations center, the men of the tank-killer teams had been searching for more LAW's. Colonel Schungel, Lieutenant Wilkins, Lieutenant Quy, and Specialist McMurray were outside the east entrance to the command bunker, crouched behind a double row of 55-gallon drums filled with rocks and earth. Sgt. (E-5) David M. Brooks, Lieutenant Longgrear, and Sergeant Fragos had gone down inside the bunker to hunt for more LAW's, but the others poured a withering fusillade of small arms fire on the enemy infantrymen to keep them from moving in on the operations center. Someone fired a rocket point-blank at the tank approaching from the direction of Company 104 but merely immobilized it. With a jolting roar the tank fired at the command bunker at a range of less than fifteen meters. The blast blinded McMurray and mangled both his hands. It hit some of the rock-filled drums, half burying Wilkins beneath them. Colonel Schungel, knocked flat by the explosion, was stunned and suffered a fragmentation wound in his hip.

On the heels of the blast, the North Vietnamese troops rushed at the small band, firing their AK47 assault rifles. But Lieutenant Quy, who was not injured, fired his M16 rifle as fast as he could reload and undoubtedly saved his companions, for once again the enemy infantrymen faltered, their ranks depleted by the deadly fire.

Regaining full consciousness, Colonel Schungel dragged the seriously injured McMurray behind a pole of sandbags at the entrance to the operations center. Wilkins, though able to dig himself out of the rubble, was still dazed. The three men held a hurried conference. Wilkins wanted to move down into the operations center but Schungel felt they would have a better chance for survival if they remained above. In any case, they had to act soon for the enemy would undoubtedly succeed in his next assault. When Lieutenant Quy suggested that they find a hiding place away from the command bunker, the two American officers agreed.

Quy ran for the team house, but as Wilkins and Schungel started to follow, the second tank that had passed Lieutenant Todd approached from the west. Schungel and Wilkins hurried back to cover just as the tank fired at the observation tower on the command bunker. The explosion caught Specialist Moreland on the ladder as he was attempting to enter the tower and wounded him. Sfc. Hugh E. Earley, who was already in the tower, suffered wounds in the head and shoulders from shell fragments.

While both injured men climbed down from the tower and into the bunker, Schungel rushed forward and tossed two hand grenades under the tank. Almost simultaneously a rocket from a LAW struck the tank in the rear. The tank commander's cupola hatch flipped open with a metallic clang, but only flames emerged. Possibly affected by the sight, the crew of the other tank attempted to leave their stalled vehicle, although it was still operable. As each crewman crawled out, Colonel Schungel killed him with an M16.

By this time North Vietnamese soldiers in small groups were all over the camp. Lieutenant Wilkins yelled down into the bunker that he and Schungel were coming down. Schungel, however, persuaded him that they would have a better chance if they were not pinned down, and the two men sought refuge in the team house.

It was 0230.

Although the enemy appeared to be all but in possession of the camp, Lang Vei's defenders had not given up. The tank attack had demolished both entrances to the deeply dug command bunker. Inside

135

were Captain Willoughby, Lieutenant Longgrear, Sergeant Brooks, S. Sgt. Emanuel E. Phillips, Sergeant Earley, Sergeant Fragos, Specialist Moreland, and Specialist Dooms, most of them wounded. With them inside were the Vietnamese camp commander (Willoughby's counterpart), the Vietnamese sergeant major, the Company 104 commander, an interpreter, a CIDG communications man, and twenty-five other Civilian Irregular Defense Group soldiers.

A few seconds after Lieutenant Longgrear had descended into the operations center with Fragos and Brooks in search of LAW's, he had heard the tank blast away at the bunker entrance above him. Longgrear, knowing where he had last seen Colonel Schungel, assumed that the colonel could not have escaped the blast and yelled to Willoughby that Schungel was dead. In the confusion of the moment, Willoughby, without questioning, accepted his death as fact. He also assumed that the only survivors left in the camp were those inside the operations center with him.

Above the bunker, Schungel and Wilkins had no sooner left for the team house than the North Vietnamese converged on the operations center. A tank rumbled onto the top of the bunker in an attempt to crush it, but the six-foot crust of dirt, steel, and reinforced concrete held. Enemy infantrymen then began to toss grenades and satchel charges and to fire their weapons down the damaged stairwells.

The wounded McMurray, whom Schungel had dragged to safety and left behind the sandbags at the entrance, yelled down the stairwell for help. Attempts to rush up the steps and rescue him were met by a burst from automatic weapons.

Willoughby extinguished all lights in the bunker. Although lack of message traffic on his radio reinforced his belief that no other team members remained in the camp above him, he was determined to hold the operations center to the end. He cautioned everyone to keep his weapon at the ready and told those who were not wounded to keep a sharp eye on the entrances, from which he expected a determined final enemy assault. But for the time being the North Vietnamese seemed content merely to harass the men below.

Above ground American and Vietnamese defenders who had escaped death or capture were trying to evade the enemy and escape. Sergeant Tirach had remained at the 4.2-inch mortar pit as long as he could. Then, with Sergeant Brooks, he had climbed to the roof of the team house, armed the .50-caliber machine gun there with armor-piercing ammunition, and was firing away at the tank attacking the bunker entrance. When the tank began sweeping Tirach's position with machine gun fire, Brooks headed for the bunker while Tirach ran for the western side of the team house. At the team house Tirach found Sfc. Michael W. Craig, Willoughby's team sergeant, Sergeant Thompson, Sergeant Burke, and about fifty CIDG and mobile strike force soldiers. After a hurried conference they decided to leave the camp through the northern perimeter— the only place where there was no visible sign of the enemy.

With little difficulty the defenders made their way quickly but cautiously through the inner barbed wire. While they were attempting to cross the triple concertina wire, heavy machine gun fire began to beat about them from the eastern section of the camp. All but Tirach, Craig, and perhaps ten Vietnamese had made it outside by this time. Taking refuge in shallow ditches, the group waited for perhaps five minutes until the artillery fire ceased and airplane illumination died down. They then slipped through the wire and ran to a clump of bamboo 100 meters away. For almost half an hour they stayed in the bamboo, until a U.S. Air Force jet dropped cluster bomb units among them, wounding Craig and Tirach. They then moved 200 meters north and finally settled in a dry creek bed which offered some cover and concealment. Around them they could hear Vietnamese voices and a continuing exchange of small arms and automatic weapons fire, while off in the distance the steady drone of tank engines and the rattling of machine gun fire, punctuated by the sharp crack and whine of artillery, told them that the fight was still raging in the camp.

When Colonel Schungel and Lieutenant Wilkins had reached the team house, Schungel directed Wilkins, who was weaponless, to hide behind the bar. The colonel then armed himself with an Ml6, two magazines, and two fragmentation grenades and took a position in the center of the building where he could observe both entrances. He had cut the inner-tube hinges from both doors so that they would remain open.

He did not have long to wait.

At 0330, five North Vietnamese infantrymen, three with AK47's and two with satchel charges, approached the northern entrance. Unsuspecting, they came toward the building in a group, chattering excitedly. Schungel signalled Wilkins to remain quiet. When the North Vietnamese were less than five meters away the colonel mowed them all down with the bullets from one magazine.

Almost immediately, a burst of small arms fire raked the room, followed by the explosion of a satchel charge which rattled the building, wounding Colonel Schungel in the right calf. Realizing the vulnerability of the team house, Schungel decided that he and Wilkins should take cover under the dispensary.

Moving quietly, they made their way to the medical building, which lay less than a hundred meters away to the west. As they crouched in the darkness under the northern end of the shack, they could hear what sounded like at least an enemy platoon inside, smashing bottles and destroying medical supplies. Between the bursts of gunfire and exploding bombs, they could also hear snatches of conversation between a runner from a battalion headquarters and an enemy company commander. Schungel and Wilkins felt safe for the moment and settled down to wait.

What was being done by higher headquarters, in the meantime, to reinforce the camp while there was still time?

Shortly after the tanks had smashed into the camp early in the fight, Willoughby had radioed the 26th Marine Regiment at Khe Sanh to comply with the reinforcement plan by sending two companies of infantrymen. The marines denied the request. They did so a second time at approximately 0330 when Willoughby tried again. When Company C headquarters learned that the request had been denied, it too tried and was turned down. The marines declined to send a relief force because they felt that any attempt to reinforce via the highway would be ambushed. A heliborne assault, they believed, was out of the question because it was dark and the enemy had armor.

While the issue was debated back and forth until it reached Headquarters, III Marine Amphibious Force, and then Military Assistance Command, Vietnam, Company C headquarters placed a mobile strike force company at Da Nang on standby alert, as well as a second company-size unit from another A detachment in the I Corps tactical zone. As soon as helicopters were available, they were to be committed.

The siege of the tactical operations center meanwhile continued and by 0320 Willoughby was unable to communicate with Da Nang directly because enemy fire had destroyed most of the radio antennas. He nevertheless continued to receive Khe Sanh loud and clear. Relaying instructions through the marines, Willoughby continued to call for air strikes and artillery.

The enemy persistently harassed the force trapped in the bunker with grenades, explosives, and bursts of fire down the stairwells. By 0430 the North Vietnamese had begun to dig a hole parallel to the wall of the operations center bunker. As the minutes ticked by Willoughby and his men could hear the muted sounds of intrenching tools clawing at the earth, and the animated chatter of the Vietnamese; from time to time someone tossed a grenade down one of the stairwells where it went off harmlessly.

Shortly after 0600 a thermite grenade rolled into the darkened command bunker and exploded in a bright orange flash before anyone could grab it. Maps and papers that were scattered about the bunker caught fire. The enemy followed this success with a flurry of fragmentation grenades and for the first time used tear gas grenades.

Though the fires burned out in twenty minutes because of poor ventilation, the smoke and gas created momentary panic. To breathe easier, the defenders hugged the floor where the air was fresher and took turns with the few gas masks they had. All became sick and many vomited. Assuming that the end was near, Phillips and Dooms began throwing classified documents into the fire. A voice called down the stairwell in Vietnamese.

"We are going to blow up the bunker, so give up now."

Coughing and sputtering as he spoke, the Vietnamese camp commander held a hurried conference with his CIDG troops, then led them up the stairs and out of the bunker. They had evidently decided to surrender.

For perhaps five minutes nothing happened. Willoughby had been depending on the firepower of the fifteen or so Vietnamese. There were eight Americans left, six of them wounded, including himself. Still he was determined to hold out.

Squinting his eyes from the smarting effect of the gas, Sergeant Fragos edged as close as he dared to the door through which the Vietnamese had just passed. Cautiously, he leaned out and peered upward. In the flare light above he could see six CIDG soldiers lined around the exit with one of the detachment's interpreters. The interpreter yelled excitedly to Fragos in English to surrender. Before Fragos could reply, a North Vietnamese soldier wearing a steel helmet with camouflaged cover and armed with an AK50 folding stock automatic weapon, tossed a grenade at him.

Fragos screamed a warning as he dived to the floor.

"Grenade!"

Other than Fragos, who was nicked in the left elbow by a small grenade fragment, no one was injured. The sergeant piled pieces of rubble and flak vests on top of himself as a shower of grenades bounced down the stairs. All exploded harmlessly.

After the explosions all was quiet except for the digging sounds, which were coming steadily closer to the wall and the talk between the CIDG troops and their captors above. Fragos moved back to the door, this time with Longgrear and Moreland. Up above they saw a North Vietnamese summarily shoot a CIDG soldier who had been stripped to his shorts. The three men eased back into the bunker as a voice called out in English from upstairs.

"We want to speak to your captain. Is he still there?"

Fragos replied defiantly, "Yes!"

"Have you got a weapon?"

"Yep!"

"Do you have ammo?"

"I've got plenty for you!"

All three fired their Ml6's up the stairwell. In response the enemy tossed down another barrage of grenades.

The talking between the captors and the South Vietnamese above the bunker stopped. And then, amidst screams and yells, the enemy soldiers began firing their weapons. Although no bodies were found later at the spot, the Americans assumed that the prisoners were executed.

It was 0630, almost dawn. As Willoughby lay there on the cold concrete floor, trying not to think of his thirst, he noticed that the digging sounds had ceased. On the other side of the north wall of the bunker he could hear Vietnamese voices. Suddenly, with an ear-splitting roar, the wall disappeared in a boiling cloud of dust and smoke, and chunks of concrete flew about the bunker. When the smoke and dust cleared, there was a gaping hole in the wall, six feet wide and four feet high. Now the North Vietnamese soldiers had direct access to the bunker.

The blast had knocked Fragos unconscious and seriously wounded Moreland in the head. Dragging both men well back from the hole, Willoughby and the others steeled themselves for the final enemy assault. Yet the North Vietnamese did not seize the advantage and seemed satisfied instead to continue tossing random hand grenades into the operations center.

Although Willoughby had no way of knowing it, efforts to relieve him were close at hand. At the old Lang Vei Camp, Sergeant Ashley, Sergeant Allen, and Specialist Johnson had continued to try to get some help for their beleaguered comrades. Turned down by the Laotian battalion commander when they had asked him for men earlier, the three Americans held him to his promise to give them troops at dawn. While they waited for first light, they directed air strikes and flare drops.

As the sky turned gray, the three Americans went again to the Laotian battalion commander. After an hour's haggling, they were able to muster perhaps 100 armed Laotians. Ashley assembled them and, through an interpreter, explained that they were going to the camp, rescue survivors, and retake the camp if possible.

While Johnson radioed Dooms in the tactical operations center that they would be on the way shortly, Ashley and Allen formed the force into a skirmish line for the move. Next, Ashley radioed the forward air controller overhead for strafing runs on the camp to soften it up. The three Americans watched as the stubby aircraft swooped down low over the camp through enemy machine gun fire, its weapons blazing. With the rescue force extended on line for approximately a hundred meters, Ashley, who was in the middle of the formation, with his PRC-25 radio strapped to his back, gave the signal to advance. To help control the maneuver, Allen was on the right flank, Johnson on the left flank.

The party ventured cautiously toward the camp, passing through what had been the Company 101 area. Several wounded CIDG and mobile strike force soldiers were sprawled among the dead North Vietnamese and the bodies of two CIDG men. A few satchel charges and weapons were scattered around. Allen stopped to exchange his carbine for a Browning automatic rifle and picked up as many magazines as he could carry and half a dozen grenades. A few minutes later the rescue party came upon some CIDG and strike force troops still in fighting condition and with little prompting the stragglers joined the force.

Approaching the eastern end of the Company 101 position, Specialist Johnson looked to his left front just in time to see two Vietnamese waving to the Laotian troops from bunkers in the Company 104 sector, less than a hundred meters away. Johnson, not wanting to take chances, yelled to them to come out of the bunkers with their hands in the air. The two soldiers ignored him and continued to wave and shout. Sensing a trap, Johnson shouted for everyone to get down, and none too soon. Almost immediately the enemy opened up with at least two machine guns and other automatic weapons.

In response to yells from the three Americans to advance, some of the Laotians inched forward reluctantly while others pulled back. Minutes passed. A shell from an 82-mm. mortar round landed so close to Johnson that the blast blew him twenty meters, though miraculously he was not wounded. After two determined efforts to organize a frontal charge proved futile, Ashley gave the order to pull back north beyond the Company 101 position to Highway 9. He would soften the target with air strikes. Ashley radioed Willoughby that he had met stiff resistance but would try again.

The time was 0800.

Inside the operations center, the Americans waited. Before Ashley's attempt, they could hear heavy enemy machine gun fire from just above them on each air strike pass. The enemy would not give up his prize easily. Meanwhile, Fragos busied himself with tending the wounded as best he could. His biggest worry was Specialist Moreland, who was delirious from a dangerous head wound. Willoughby worked at his radio, trying to re-establish communication with Khe Sanh which he had just lost a few minutes before. A grenade sailed through the hole in the wall, knocking him unconscious.

Now leaderless, the Americans decided to play dead in the hope that the enemy would go away. Fragos, administering morphine to Moreland to calm him, was overcome by nausea from the gas fumes, acrid smoke, and lack of water, and started to vomit. Specialist Dooms stopped his work on the radio to quiet him as the waiting game with the enemy continued. The men spoke only when necessary and then in brief whispers.

Outside the bunker, Colonel Schungel and Lieutenant Wilkins had remained beneath the dispensary undetected all night. With the approach of dawn, the colonel still elected to remain hidden; the heavy firing convinced him that it would be folly to attempt to escape at this point. From their hiding place, the two men listened to air strikes that Sergeant Ashley had called in to blast the camp. By about 0930 when the strikes were over, they cautiously hobbled out from under the dispensary and headed east. Just west of the building were the hulks of two burned out tanks, apparently destroyed by aircraft. Seeing an air controller circling above, Schungel waved frantically. The pilot waggled his wings in acknowledgment. At this point, Schungel was convinced that he and Wilkins were the only ones left alive in the camp.

As they passed through the 1st Combat Reconnaissance Platoon positions, there was no sign of life. Finding an abandoned Upton truck, Schungel tried in vain to start it. While he and Wilkins were tinkering with the engine a Vietnamese yelled to them from a nearby bunker to join him. Glad to know that there were still some friendly troops alive, the two exhausted Americans limped toward the bunker. As Wilkins entered, Schungel, who was just behind him, fell with a bullet in his right thigh. He had been wounded for the third time.

Unlike Colonel Schungel and Lieutenant Wilkins, Sergeant Tirach and the others in his group had ventured from their hiding places just north of the camp shortly after dawn and were cautiously edging their way eastward toward Khe Sanh. Observing Ashley's first abortive assault on the camp and assuming that it was a friendly action, they came out in the open, waving and shouting to attract attention. When they were not fired upon, they moved closer. Sergeant Tirach got the scare of his life when he was near enough to see that many of the men in the attacking force carried AK47 assault rifles, the standard weapon of the North Vietnamese. He did not know that the Laotians often used enemy weapons. Stepping out on the road to get a better look, Sergeant Tirach was relieved to see Ashley at the radio, with Johnson and Allen nearby. When Ashley explained what they were trying to do, Tirach and his men, for all their fatigue, readily agreed to help.

During the second assault the enemy used 81-mm. and 60-mm. mortars against the American-led force. As the Americans approached closer the North Vietnamese, yelling and screaming, began tossing grenades and firing automatic weapons. On one flank the force came to within twenty-five meters of the enemy-held bunkers before some of the Laotians again began to fall back.

While Ashley called in air strikes, Tirach caught sight of Colonel Schungel limping toward the group along Highway 9 with the aid of two CIDG soldiers; three others were helping Lieutenant Wilkins. Running to the wounded colonel, Tirach and Allen carried him to the attacking group's assembly area, a spot perhaps 500 meters west of the old camp, just off the highway.

Ashley then lifted the air strike and radioed the operations center bunker that he would try again. The rescue force had dwindled to half its original size. Allen and Ashley had to force Craig, who had been shot in the hip, to remain behind.

For the third time, the men advanced frontally against the enemy bunker line. Johnson and Tirach remained behind to man a 60-mm. mortar with which they lobbed high-explosive shells and one white phosphorus round into the enemy positions just ahead. The seventh round misfired. Cursing their luck, Johnson and Tirach snatched up their own weapons and joined the assault. The attackers made good progress until the enemy let go with a fusillade of small arms fire from the bunkers. Puffs of smoke rose from exploding hand grenades. Again the attack failed.

Determined to try once more, Ashley radioed the forward air controller to plaster the area again and to continue the strikes, shifting them westward, just ahead of his assault line as it advanced. He yelled to Johnson to return to the old camp for a 57-mm. recoilless rifle. With it he could perhaps knock out the bunkers.

As the aircraft darted down on their bombing and strafing runs, Allen watched them from where he lay sprawled in the dust, catching his breath. He felt certain that this time the attackers could reach the operations center. He had counted only nine enemy soldiers during the last assault and had even seen a few of those hit. With the added firepower of the recoilless rifle, one determined charge would do the job.

As Ashley and his men assaulted for the fourth time, Johnson sighted and aimed the recoilless rifle for the Vietnamese gunner. Too anxious, the gunner jerked the trigger and the round went high, missing the entire camp. Impatiently, Johnson pulled the nervous gunner aside, and with another CIDG soldier loading for him put three high-explosive rounds in the front aperture of each of the two bunkers that had been giving the attackers the most trouble. Turning the weapon over to the gunner, he raced forward to join the assault.

The added firepower obviously helped, for the attackers passed through the bunker line. They had reached the easternmost 81-mm. mortar pit and quickened their pace for a dash to the operations bunker when Ashley fell. A bullet had passed through his chest on the right side and gone through the radio on his back. The North Vietnamese soldiers had plenty of fight left in them and cut loose with everything they had. The attack again collapsed.

Running to the fallen Ashley, Johnson and Allen managed to drag him out of the line of fire, and with the aid of CIDG soldiers they carried him back to the assembly area. A jeep from the old camp arrived and the soldiers loaded the seriously wounded sergeant into the back. As the jeep bounced along the dusty road, Johnson administered mouth-to-mouth respiration to Ashley. Finally the jeep ground to a halt. No sooner had Allen leaped from it to run in search of bandages than an enemy artillery round burst nearby, killing Ashley and knocking Johnson unconscious. (Ashley was posthumously awarded the Medal of Honor.)

This last blow came at 1110 and marked the end of attempts to reach the trapped force in the operations bunker.

At Da Nang, in the meantime, the matter of how to reinforce the camp was still under discussion. When the commander of the Military Assistance Command, Vietnam, General William C. Westmoreland, who happened to be in Da Nang at the time for a conference, learned of the fight and the marines' decision not to risk a relief force, he directed the marines to supply enough helicopters for a fifty-man mobile strike force under Special Forces control. He also directed Col. Jonathan F. Ladd, commanding officer of the Special Forces Group, and Maj. Gen. Norman J. Anderson, commanding officer of the 1st Marine Air Wing, to develop a rescue plan. The survivors were to be brought out, for, although no official report had been received, the Lang Vei Special Forces Camp had apparently fallen to the enemy.

In the command bunker at the Lang Vei Camp, Captain Willoughby had regained consciousness during Ashley's final assault. When the attack failed, he called the survivors together. Occasional grenades were still being tossed into the bunker, and the men could hear enemy weapons firing above them. It was getting late and they had been without food or water for almost eighteen hours. Convinced that no help was on the way, Willoughby told the men that he would radio for all available air strikes and that afterward they would make a break for it. Because Moreland was mortally wounded and the others in their injured and exhausted condition would have had difficulty carrying him, the decision was made by all to leave Moreland in the bunker. Willoughby planned to return for him later.

When Willoughby radioed for air strikes, the air controller replied by directing salvo after salvo on the positions. Shock waves beat against the faces of the survivors as heavy percussion shook the ground underneath them. At 1600 the men were ready. With Lieutenant Longgrear in the lead, one at a time they quietly climbed the stairs and then ran for supply bunker Number 2. Overhead, planes flew dummy passes to keep the enemy covered up.

As Fragos, the sixth man out, neared the supply bunker, automatic weapons fire from the former positions of Company 104 began to beat a deadly path in the dirt just fifty meters ahead of him.

Lieutenant Longgrear wheeled and fired an entire magazine from his M16 rifle into the bunker aperture, silencing the weapon. With Sergeant Phillips and Captain Willoughby carrying Sergeant Earley, the men made their way out of the camp unmolested.

A few meters east of the perimeter, Lieutenant Quy in a jeep met them and everyone piled in. When the survivors reached the old camp Willoughby found Colonel Schungel, in spite of his wounds, hard at work on the radios, trying to co-ordinate the arrival of the fifty-man evacuation force. Willoughby told him that as far as he knew there were no survivors outside of the operations center. Schungel in turn radioed the forward air controller to plaster the entire camp with bombs, except for the tactical operations center.

Although the men did not know it, Lieutenant Todd was still in the Lang Vei Camp. During the afternoon he too had realized it was now or never, and shortly after Willoughby's band had escaped he himself had left the emergency medical bunker. He drew automatic weapons fire that came from behind him as he went first to the operations center, hoping to find some Americans still alive. Instead, he found Moreland inside, apparently dead, half-buried in debris from a direct bomb hit on the operations center. As he left the bunker he looked in the direction of the old camp just in time to see one of the rescue helicopters land there. Elated, the lieutenant, despite his wound, ran to the old camp.

When Todd arrived, the rescue operation was well in progress. A flight of Marine Huey gunships and jet aircraft was circling the area to provide cover. The fifty-man reaction force had established a perimeter around the landing zone. By 1730 all known survivors had been evacuated to Khe Sanh.

The battle for Lang Vei was over. Of an original fighting force of approximately 500 indigenous troops, Captain Willoughby had lost over 200 killed or missing and 75 wounded. Out of 24 Americans, 10 were killed or missing and 11 wounded. Almost all the camp's weapons; and equipment were completely destroyed.

Nearly 6,000 stragglers from the Lang Vei area, Laotian soldiers, mountain tribesmen, South Vietnamese irregulars, and nondescript civilians—followed Willoughby's men to Khe Sanh. When the panicky horde descended on the Marine base, its commander Col. David Lownds, knowing that enemy agents might well have mingled with the crowd, refused to admit the refugees. Instead, he took away their weapons and held the refugees in an area outside the wire. Eventually representatives of the American Special Forces were called in to screen them and evacuate those whom the Special Forces determined to be friendly.

Thus did Lang Vei fall, marking the first successful use of armor by the enemy in the Vietnam War. There were those who believed that the loss of the camp would eventually lead to the destruction of Khe Sanh, but these fears never materialized.

7. Gunship Mission
5 May 1968

BY JOHN A. CASH

By mid-1966 gun helicopter platoons, each platoon consisting of eight UH-1 (Huey) helicopters armed with rockets and machine guns and each platoon organic to an assault helicopter company were hard at work all over South Vietnam. Usually five of the Hueys in a platoon were kept ready at all times while the other three were held in reserve or were undergoing maintenance. Four of the ready gunships flew in pairs, designated light fire teams. The fifth could be used to augment the fire of either team, and when so employed the three ships constituted a heavy fire team. Operating in support of American, South Vietnamese, and allied forces, these fire teams had a hazardous assignment, for the relatively slow-moving helicopter, flying at low levels, is highly vulnerable to ground fire. So valuable was the ships' support to ground troops, however, that the risks were considered justifiable.

In the spring of 1968 an incident occurred on the outskirts of Saigon, the South Vietnamese capital that illustrates some of the methods used by the fire teams. (See Map 1 on page 8)

The strong offensive launched by the North Vietnamese and the Viet Cong during the Tet holiday had ended, but intelligence sources indicated the possibility of a follow-up assault against the capital. During late April and the first few days of May, substantial enemy forces were reported moving closer to Saigon from three directions.

To meet the enemy threat, Maj. Gen. Le Nguyen Khang, the South Vietnamese Army commander responsible for the defense of the city, relocated his forces, which normally operated in the outlying areas surrounding Saigon, to form a defensive ring closer to the city. As a part of the new deployment, he installed the three battalions of the South Vietnamese 5th Ranger Group on the edge of the Cholon sector in southwestern Saigon. General Khang charged his units with locating enemy caches, preventing infiltration of men, weapons, ammunition,

Viet Cong bodies in a ditch in the French National Cemetery on the southwest perimeter of Tan Son Nhut Air Bas, killed by gunships.

and equipment, and destroying any enemy forces that might manage to slip in.

The 5th Ranger Group, to carry out this order, placed two companies of its 30th Ranger Battalion in approximately thirty ambush positions along a north-south line a few kilometers west of the Phu Tho Racetrack, in the center of the Cholon sector, with another company behind them as a blocking force. A fourth company continued to perform security duties at the battalion base camp, eight kilometers away.

In addition to reinforcements available from II Field Force and Vietnamese III Corps headquarters and on-call artillery arid air strikes, General Khang's units could ask for assistance from the gunships of the 120th Aviation Company (Airmobile, Light). At that point in the Vietnam fighting, the 120th Aviation Company was not engaged in the combat assaults usually performed by such units but was assigned to provide administrative transportation for headquarters of the Military Assistance Command, Vietnam (MACV), and headquarters of the United States Army, Vietnam (USARV). In April 1968, however, MACV headquarters had directed that four armed helicopters of the company's gunship platoon be made available to Capital Military District headquarters to provide fire support for ground troops in and around Saigon. One fire team was to be on 5-minute alert status on the Air Force flight line at Tan Son Nhut Air Base while the other was to be on 30-minute standby at the gunship platoon headquarters on the Tan Son Nhut Air Base helipad. These gunships of the 120th Aviation Company were later to become heavily involved in the defense of Saigon against a major enemy attack.

Before dawn on 5 May 1968 the enemy offensive erupted. A battalion of a main force Viet Cong regiment with an estimated strength of 300 men attacked the Newport Bridge and adjacent docking facilities along the waterfront in northeastern Saigon.

The fight was joined.

A half-hour later two battalions of the 271st Main Force Viet Cong Regiment, followed by another regiment, attacked eastward in the 5th Ranger Group's Cholon sector. Using small arms, automatic weapons, and rocket fire, they attempted to seize the headquarters of the 6th Police Precinct. Throughout the morning, the 30th Ranger Battalion was heavily engaged with forces of the 3d Battalion, 271st Viet Cong Regiment, less than 3,000 meters due west of the Phu Tho Racetrack. Although the rangers had managed to slow the enemy with artillery and helicopter assistance, the fight was stiff raging in the early afternoon; hardest hit was the 3d Company, which was pinned down and under attack by two enemy companies.

Around 1400 the 30th Battalion's commander asked his American adviser, Capt. Roland L. Petit, a 27-year-old infantry officer, for help. The 3d Company, he said, had already lost six dead and ten wounded.

Captain Petit, an experienced adviser, considered the situation.

Artillery thus far had apparently had a negligible effect on the determined enemy force. Furthermore, Petit knew from his Tet offensive experience that in deference to the civilian population General Khang would authorize tactical air strikes in or near the city only when all else had failed. There was but one thing left, Captain Petit reasoned—another gunship run. He radioed the request, his fifth of the day, to Capital Military District headquarters.

When his message crackled over the operation radio at headquarters of the 120th Aviation Company Gunship Platoon a few moments later, Maj. James P. Hunt, the platoon leader and veteran of 500 hours and 19 months of combat flying in Vietnam, had just finished inspecting his helicopters on the ready line at the Tan Son Nhut helipad. In the sweltering heat of this Sunday afternoon, he was about to feast on a C ration meal of pork steak. So far it had been a rough day. Hunt's five helicopters were riddled with bullet holes and that morning he had lost two crewmen wounded by ground fire. Furthermore, he knew that the others in his platoon were at least as tired as he was, since they had been flying fire support missions without letup for South Vietnamese marines and rangers since 0500. Yet he still had two fire teams operational as required, one on 5-minute alert at the Air Force flight line, the other on 30-minute standby at platoon headquarters.

Acknowledging the message, Hunt turned to Warrant Officer Ronald W. Davis, one of his 30-minute standby pilots. Davis, still in his sweat-soaked flying suit, was sprawled on the ground, legs stretched out, back against the wall, half asleep with fatigue. "Crank up your ship, Ron. We've got a mission near the racetrack again for our ranger friends. I'll fly the right seat with you and fill you in when we're airborne."

"Roger, sir." Davis got to his feet slowly and buckled on his .45-caliber pistol. Wiping the sweat from his forehead with the back of his hand, he walked toward his helicopter. Davis, in Hunt's opinion, was one of his best pilots. He himself would accompany Davis because the co-pilot had been put out of action earlier that morning when enemy rifle fire shattered the plexiglass windshield and smashed his ankle.

Asleep on a bench a few feet away lay Maj. Chadwick C. Payne, who would pilot the other helicopter. Hunt nudged him gently.

"Let's go, Chad. We've got another one."

At the helipad some yards away from the operations building, Davis found Spec. 5 Dennis A. Sullivan, his 20-year-old, bespectacled, soft-spoken crew chief, and Spec. 4 Fred L. Rexer, his husky door gunner. Both men were stripped to the waist in the shimmering heat, reloading their gunship with ammunition to replace that which had been expended on a previous mission. Davis told them to get ready for a take-off in the next few minutes and then began his own preflight check.

Davis' helicopter mounted the XM16 weapons system, consisting of two externally mounted 7.62-mm. M60CA1 machine guns ("flexguns") and fourteen 2.75-inch folding-fin aerial rockets, seven on each side of the ship. Capable of a cyclic rate of fire of 2,400 rounds per minute per machine gun, the M60CA1's had been designed to allow for an increased rate of 4,000 rounds per minute on the outboard gun when either was traversed to its inboard limit and stopped firing. In addition, the flexguns were controlled by a 3-second maximum fire time, with a momentary delay between firings. The rockets could be fired singly, in pairs, or in salvos from their cylindrical pods to a maximum effective range of 2,500 meters for area targets. They were most effective against point targets at 200 to 500 meters.

Specialist Sullivan inserted the last of the fourteen rockets in its chamber and then double-checked each of the 10-pound missiles to insure that all were loaded with secure detents in the twin mounts.

Specialist Rexer, who had been shot in the leg on an earlier mission, was a veteran of twenty-one months' combat in Vietnam, including infantry duty, and knew well what to do. He reloaded the twelve feeder ammunition boxes located in the cargo compartment with 6,000 rounds of 7.62-mm. machine gun bullets and stacked 2,000 rounds each for his door gun and Sullivan's. Satisfying himself that the ammunition rack-to-helicopter cable assembly was secure, he placed the rack firing switch to the reset position and continued his preflight check.

Chewing on an unlit cigar and scratching at a day-old growth of beard, Major Payne arrived at his ship on the revested stand next to Davis'. He began his preflight check, assisted by his crew of three.

Payne would be piloting the "big gun" of the team, a helicopter outfitted with the deadly XM3 armament system comprising two externally mounted pods, each containing twenty-four rockets that could be fired in the same manner as those of the other gunship.

Unlike Davis' ship, however, Payne's carried no machine guns other than the usual two manned by the crew chief and door gunner.

Satisfied with the preparations, Major Hunt donned his crash helmet and body armor, climbed into the pilot's seat of Davis' helicopter, and prepared for take-off. As Davis went about his preflight check in the co-pilot's seat, Hunt adjusted his own safety belt and shoulder harness and began to assist. Within minutes the checks were completed, the engine throbbed at idle, and Hunt and his three companions, along with Payne and his crew, awaited take-off clearance instructions from the helipad tower.

While he waited, Hunt radioed Payne, with Davis monitoring, and explained that they would be flying in support of the rangers again, in the same general area in which they had flown that morning. Other than that hostile fire was rampant in the area, Hunt could tell them nothing. The size of the enemy force and its exact location on the ground would have to come later. Actually, except for briefing them when he learned the enemy position, Hunt would have no need to issue further instructions to Payne or Davis, for standing operating procedure, along with the experience of weeks of flying together as a team, dictated the tactical techniques that would be used once the target was identified.

After a 5-minute wait, the tower cleared Payne's team for takeoff. With a less than 5-knot southwest-northeast crosswind and unlimited visibility, Payne chose to use the normal vertical take-off-to-hover-and-then-climb procedure. He led out first, with Hunt's ship a few hundred meters behind.

Engines roaring, the two helicopters climbed to 1,500 feet above Tan Son Nhut and then headed in a southeasterly direction. In a few minutes they were over the junction of the Saigon River and its southwest tributary, which bordered the city. Turning to the southwest they followed the muddy stream until they reached a point perhaps five kilometers southwest of the Phu Tho Racetrack, where both ships circled while Hunt switched to Captain Petit's radio frequency.

"I'm getting up pretty close to your position," Major Hunt said. "Where are you? Over."

As Petit answered, the noise of heavy small arms fire could be heard in the background. "I've got you in sight. We've been receiving heavy fire all morning and this afternoon. Hold on station at your orbit while

I double-check our artillery check fire. Over."

"Roger, dodger. Standing by." Both Hunt and Payne monitored Petit's instructions and continued to maneuver their ships in a tight circle, staying clear of the artillery gun target line. Volleys of high-explosive shells fired from the Phu Tho Racetrack, their bright orange explosions lost in the glare of the afternoon sun, were slamming into the target area. It would be hazardous to attempt a gun run.

Hunt radioed Petit again. "Where's all the action? Over."

"It's at coordinates X-RAY SIERRA SEVEN NINER ZERO, EIGHT NINER NINER. OVER."

Hunt wanted to be sure. "Say again those co-ordinates. Over."

"Right down there where you fired on that factory earlier, where you had the individual wounded this morning. Over."

Listening to the interchange, Payne knew as well as Hunt exactly where to look. Neither could forget the deadly hail of fire which had met the ships on each pass that morning and had wounded Davis' co-pilot.

The target area lay to the north of the gunships on the outskirts of the city, two kilometers due west of the racetrack. A built-up factory complex of one-story brick buildings, dominated by a tall pagoda, bordered the west side of a north-south all-weather road. A few hundred meters to the west stood Ap Tan Hoi, perhaps one kilometer square, surrounded by rice fields. Under a thick pall of smoke, much of the hamlet lay in ruins from artillery fire and the northeast corner was in flames, evidence of the heavy fighting in progress between the Viet Cong and the 3d Company of the 30th Ranger Battalion.

Again Hunt radioed Petit. "Are you on the west side of the road, in and along those low brick buildings? Over."

"Negative! Negative on that! To the west of the road you'll see a pagoda about 200 meters from it. Including the pagoda and north of the pagoda, all those low buildings belong to you. Suggest you approach from the east. Over."

"Roger," answered Hunt. "Understand the pagoda and north of it belongs to me, but negative on an east approach. We got a lot of ground fire over there when we did that this morning. We'll be approaching from the west. Over."

Petit acknowledged. He would have preferred the gunships to attack from the east, for other ranger units were deployed east of the road.

Nevertheless, he could understand Hunt's decision. The pilot wanted to attack from a new direction to avoid setting a pattern and he naturally wanted the mission to go with minimum exposure of his crew members.

Petit continued. "O.K. But I'd like you to be careful. We have a friendly element in that area. Over."

"Where? Near the pagoda, north of it, or what? Over."

"Negative. Four hundred meters east of the pagoda on an east-west line. Over."

Upon hearing this Major Hunt was even more convinced that his choice of direction for the attack was sound; he would not be firing over the heads of friendly troops on the ground, always a dangerous procedure. He continued to scrutinize the target area

It would be a point target mission and he would employ running fire at a 15-degree dive angle, thus producing a relatively small beaten zone. The only disadvantages to this approach would be the increased time of exposure of each helicopter to hostile fire and the fact that the long axis of the beaten zone in this case would be perpendicular instead of coincidental to the long axis of the target. Hunt decided on his concept and told Payne about it.

"O.K., Chad. We'll work over the pagoda and around it initially, and then we'll work away from it, northward, breaking to the northwest. Got it?"

"Roger," radioed Payne. "But let's make sure we're looking at the same pagoda. I see another one not too far behind it at a greater range. Let's be sure, Jim. Over."

Again Hunt queried Petit. "Is this pagoda we're talking about on the west side of the road?"

"That's affirm. You'll see an abandoned truck out on the road in front of it. Over."

Both pilots searched for the vehicle but to no avail.

"I can't see the vehicle from this angle but I believe it's a yellow or cream-colored pagoda, isn't it?"

"That's affirm."

"Are you still picking up a lot of fire down there? Over."

"Enough."

"From the pagoda itself?" Hunt wanted him to be as precise as possible.

Anxious to get the mission started, Petit replied, "We're receiving an awful lot of small arms fire from the general area. You can start anytime and the artillery has been turned off. Over."

"No sweat. We'll start our run at this time. Out."

Both ships began to unwind from the circling position. Payne's rocket ship would go first, followed by Hunt's, with Hunt to begin firing as soon as Payne broke to the northwest. Payne would fire his rockets in six 2-round volleys on each of four passes. Co-ordinated flight on his part was of considerable importance, for if not properly streamlined in the relatively minor crosswind complete accuracy would be impossible. He estimated the target engagement range at 1,500 meters and decided to aim at the base of the pagoda for his first strike. By attacking at this range, he would be able to avoid breaking over the target area and exposing the ships to more hostile fire than necessary.

Swinging in a wide arc westward, Payne dropped to an altitude of 1,200 feet and lined up on an almost due east-west axis with the target at 90 knots, a good attack speed.

As with all rocket ship armament systems, the pilot would both fly the aircraft and fire the missiles. Payne eased over into his dive angle, switched the rocket selector switch to "two," and then turned the armament system main switch to the "armed" position. He fixed the target through the infinity sight mounted directly in front of him and as the pagoda loomed ever closer in the reticle pressed the firing button slowly three times.

The helicopter shuddered as the rockets left it. From the pagoda base black smoke rose and masonry fragments flew in all directions while Payne's two door gunners laced the area just forward of the target with M60 fire. The helicopter banked sharply left at a range of 750 meters.

Following 500 meters to the rear and slightly to the right, Major Hunt began lining up on the target axis even before Payne had made his break, for it was his job at this point to protect the exposed underside of Payne's ship from enemy fire. His co-pilot, Warrant Officer Davis, fired the flexguns, adjusting the bullet strikes into the base of the pagoda in much the same fashion as one would direct a stream of water from a garden hose. Hunt fired his rockets in two 2-round volleys, guiding on the bullet strikes, while Rexer and Sullivan fired their door guns at enemy weapons flashes and likely positions along

Rockets from Major Payne's gunship hit enemy positions

the flanks and forward of the target area.

Petit radioed his satisfaction. "You're doing a fine job. Keep it up. Did you receive any fire on that approach? Over."

Having counted at least three automatic weapons flashes in the target zone, Hunt replied, "Roger that."

Petit had a suggestion. "On your next pass you might try at the edge of the wood line and work on the same axis you just flew, up through those buildings and into the pagoda. Over."

"I assume you mean on the west side of the road. Right?"

"That's affirm."

"Roger-roger. We'll just march it a little shorter—about 200 meters short of the pagoda on up into it."

"Good," replied Petit. "We've got about an enemy squad, at least, identified in that area."

The two gunships made their second pass, approaching from the same general direction but a few degrees further southward. They received moderate fire from enemy ground positions as each ship broke.

Following this pass, Petit noticed a slackening of enemy fire. He radioed Hunt. "Your pattern is good. Keep it up."

"Roger."

As his team swung around in a wide arc for the third pass, Hunt

Major Hunt's gunship burns after landing

asked, "Can we be specific? Where is most of the enemy fire coming from, the factory buildings or the pagoda? Over."

Petit still wasn't sure. "It may be coming from either the pagoda or the factories. It's in that area in there and I understand now that there may be a platoon in there. Over."

"Roger. O.K. Real fine."

On the third pass, once again from the same general direction, the Viet Cong took the ships under fire.

Petit inquired. "Did you receive heavy fire from the target?"

"Some, but it didn't seem very intense."

As Hunt's helicopter banked to the left on his fourth pass, four rounds of enemy automatic weapons fire smashed into the bottom of the fuselage. The bullets ruptured the hydraulic system, ripped through the flexgun ammunition boxes, and lodged in the ceiling of the cargo compartment.

Leaning over to determine the extent of the damage, Specialist Sullivan could see through the bullet holes that flames were dancing around beneath the compartment floor near the fuel cell. On the intercom he told Hunt: "We're on fire, sir."

As if to second the motion, Warrant Officer Davis, having smelled the smoke, yelled, "There's a fire on here!"

Major Hunt had realized his aircraft was hit, for he had felt the impact of the rounds on the ship and almost immediately had difficulty in trying to level off from his bank, a sure sign to him that the hydraulic system had failed. The "Master Caution" light flashed on the instrument panel and a steady, piercing, high-pitched signal filled the intercom system, warning all aboard of an in-flight emergency. Hunt's immediate impulse was to head for Tan Son Nhut, a few kilometers away, but because of the fire he elected to try for a forced landing before the flames reached the fuel cell.

Davis yelled to Hunt: "Get the power down, sir! Get the power down!" He wanted to auto-rotate, that is, to make a power-off descent.

"Never mind that," Hunt replied. "Help me with the controls." He needed all the help he could get to maneuver the ship safely to earth.

Searching frantically for a place to land, Major Hunt spotted a dry rice field a kilometer or two north of Ap Tan Hoi; it looked deserted and would afford at least 100 meters of slide space once the helicopter touched ground. With Davis assisting at the controls, Hunt executed a slow, descending, turning glide toward the field. Autorotation was out; it would have required a last-minute hover, an impossibility with the hydraulic system gone. By this time hydraulic fluid was spilling across the cabin floor and the cockpit was filling with smoke. Hunt radioed Major Payne his predicament and his plan and reported that no one had been injured.

Payne immediately swung his helicopter around and followed the crippled ship. He had no doubt that, barring a midair explosion, Major Hunt could land his craft safely. As to what to expect once it landed, Payne wasn't sure. The enemy situation was vague. Although Payne had expended all his rockets; he still had 300 rounds left for each of his door guns in the event Hunt ran into trouble. He radioed Capital Military District headquarters the situation and was promised that a rescue helicopter would soon be en route. Headquarters diverted two F-100 aircraft to orbit near on a standby basis. Alerted as well was the 5-minute standby gunship team.

Hunt and Davis continued to maneuver their helicopter toward the rice field; while behind them Specialist Rexer calmly unbuckled his safety belt, climbed outside the ship, and edged along the landing skid until he reached a point close to the pilot's compartment. He unlatched Major Hunt's door to clear away some of the smoke, then reached inside and slid the side armor protective plate rearward in order to allow the pilot a rapid exit once the ship touched down. Reaching beneath Hunt's seat with one hand and holding precariously to the side of the ship with the other, he removed the portable fire extinguisher, returned with it along the skid to the cargo compartment, and attempted to extinguish the blaze.

Specialist Sullivan also moved out onto the skid on his side, unfastened Davis' door, and returned to his own position.

Maintaining an approach speed of seventy knots, both pilots gradually applied as much control as they could in an effort to achieve a flat landing.

Skimming scrub brush and rice paddy dikes, the smoking helicopter slammed into the ground, skids first, and then slid for fifty meters before coming to a halt just short of a 3-foot rice paddy embankment. A north-south road ran perpendicular to the embankment and some 200 meters to the north a South Vietnamese Popular Forces compound was visible. The ship had come down on the east side of the road.

Even before the helicopter came to a stop, its crew went into action. Hunt and Davis shut down the engine and turned off all switches. The tank still had 800 pounds of fuel but Rexer had used up his fire extinguisher in the cargo compartment. Rexer rushed forward, grabbed Davis under the armpits, and yanked him from the co-pilot's seat. He then lent a hand to Major Hunt.

With everyone out of the aircraft, the pilots, still burdened by their cumbersome body armor, headed for a field across the road to the west that Hunt had spotted. If any of the enemy were nearby, rice stalks and tall grass offered some concealment for Hunt's men. Rexer and Sullivan, figuring there was yet time to salvage some equipment from the ship, grabbed their tools from the kits and worked against the fire that was still burning in the cargo and engine compartments. Rexer was unscrewing the flexgun pod mount assembly; Sullivan, on his knees at the front of the helicopter, had raised the access door to the electronic equipment and was dismantling the radios.

Hunt, reconnoitering the field on the west side of the road, was startled by a flash of light from the helicopter. He saw then that burning hydraulic fluid dripping from the aircraft had started a fire in the grass under the ship. It was a sudden flare-up of this fire that had caught his eye.

Downed crew leaves Popular Forces Compound for rescue helicopter

"The ship's going! Get 'em away from there!"

Davis ran toward the road, yelling to Rexer and Sullivan to pull back. The two left the plane reluctantly and headed for the road. They had just reached the embankment when the helicopter erupted into a bright orange fireball. As they watched, the fireball dissipated and the ship burned fiercely. Billows of thick black smoke rose from it and machine gun ammunition exploded in all directions.

Hunt looked at his watch. It was 1450 and they had been on the ground seven minutes. He took stock of their situation. Both Rexer and Sullivan carried M16 rifles, snatched from the ship at the last minute. Between them they had twenty-two magazines of ammunition. Hunt and Davis had .45-caliber automatics and a total of seventy-five rounds. It was not much to set up a defense. As yet no enemy had appeared, but if a force was sent to investigate the crash Hunt figured it would come from Ap Tan Hoi, a hamlet some 1,000 meters to the southwest. He ordered Sullivan and Rexer to divide their ammunition and take up positions fifty meters apart, lying prone in the field, facing south. Hunt himself took a position fifty meters inside the field—at the apex of the triangle. Davis, the co-pilot, Hunt ordered out to patrol to the west to a distance of about twenty-five meters.

During the ten minutes since Hunt's helicopter had landed, Payne, piloting the other ship in the fire team, had been hovering above.

He now decided to take a chance and land. As soon as Payne set his ship down, Hunt was beside him. Above the roar of the blades, Hunt yelled that everything was all right. Satisfied, Payne took off again. He would hover at a low level and if a rescue ship did not arrive soon he would land again and attempt to evacuate the crew himself, despite the danger inherent in the added weight of Hunt and his crew.

Davis had meanwhile returned from his patrol. He called Hunt's attention to the Popular Forces compound, 200 meters to the north. Someone in the compound was waving at them.

"See if you can signal them to come down here," said Hunt.

But the Vietnamese seemed to be waving them to come to the compound instead.

Hunt thought it over for a minute. He had no relish for staying in the open till a rescue ship arrived. He led his men, single file, toward the compound. At the gate they were welcomed by a smiling Vietnamese who seemed to be in charge.

Once inside the barbed-wire gate, the crew was surrounded by a shouting, cheering squad of Vietnamese. One soldier poured iced tea into small porcelain cups and handed them around to the Americans, bowing ceremoniously as he did so.

Ten minutes later an Air Force rescue helicopter landed just outside the gate of the compound, picked up the crewmen, and flew them back to Tan Son Nhut Air Base.

Within an hour of their return, Hunt and his crew were flying another gunship mission in a replacement aircraft. It was all in a day's work.

Glossary

ACAV Armored cavalry assault vehicle (M113 armored personnel carrier, modified for use in Vietnam)

AK47 Russian-designed assault rifle, 7.62-mm.

Area target Target for gunfire or bombing covering a considerable space, such as a munitions factory, airport, or freight yard

ARVN Army of the Republic of Vietnam

ATC Armored troop carrier (modified landing craft)

BAR Browning automatic rifle

Beaten zone The elliptical ground area struck by the fire of automatic weapons or by artillery projectiles

Beehive round An artillery or recoilless rifle round containing thousands of small darts, or flechettes

Bn Battalion

CIDG Civilian Irregular Defense Group

Co Company

CP Command post

CRP Combat reconnaissance platoon

Flexgun 7.62-mm. M60CA1 machine gun

G-2 Military intelligence section of the general staff of a large unit

Huey UH-1D helicopter

LAW M72, light assault weapon, one-shot, disposable launcher container, loaded with a shaped charge round and fired from the shoulder

LZ Landing zone

MACV Military Assistance Command, Vietnam

Minigun 7.62-mm. Gatling-type gun

Monitor Gunboat armed with 20- and 40-mm. guns and 81-mm. direct fire mortars

NVA North Vietnamese Army

OP Observation post

Plt Platoon

Point target A target which requires the accurate placement of bombs or fire

S-2 Officer in charge of the military intelligence section of a brigade or smaller unit

S-3 Officer in charge of the operations and training section of a brigade or smaller unit

S-4 Officer in charge of the supply and evacuation section of a brigade or smaller unit

Spooky AC-47 aircraft with three 7.62-mm. Gatling-type guns and illumination flares

USARV United States Army, Vietnam

www.ingramcontent.com/pod-product-compliance
Lightning Source LLC
LaVergne TN
LVHW090116080426
835507LV00040B/904